Handbook of
Professional Selling and Sales Negotiation

Simon Adams

**The Chartered
Institute of Marketing**

To Ann for her help, patience and encouragement

PITMAN PUBLISHING
128 Long Acre, London WC2E 9AN
Tel: +44 (0) 171 447 2000
Fax: +44 (0) 171 240 5771

A Division of Pearson Professional Limited

First published in Great Britain 1996

British Library Cataloguing in Publication Data
A CIP catalogue record for this book can be obtained from the British Library.

ISBN 0 273 62579 9

Typeset by Phoenix Photosetting, Chatham, Kent
Printed and bound in Great Britain by Redwood Books

The Publishers' policy is to use paper manufactured from sustainable forests.

Contents

Introduction

From the dawn of mankind, if one person had a product or service that another desired, the opportunity for a sale existed. A profession evolved, which is today the cornerstone of any commercial enterprise.

Over the last two decades, the whole process and approach to selling has changed fundamentally. No longer is it the province of the sales person, employed to convince the customer that the product or service which their company is offering is the one that they should purchase, with little or no regard to the question 'What does the customer want or need?'

> Marketing conceives and selling implements.

As world-wide competition grew, manufacturers and suppliers began to recognise the importance of considering the needs of the customer. The development of marketing disciplines emerged as a critical stage in the selling process.

Selling and negotiation have now been recognised as functions requiring a high level of skill without which few if any companies will survive in any competitive environment. Professional sales personnel, operating with the highest levels of integrity, have never been in greater demand.

The aim of this book is that it is used as a work of reference to help clarify or develop skills in specific areas and to give a greater understanding of the principles of professional selling and sales negotiation. Each subject in itself could be the basis of a book in its own right. Having grasped the basic principles you may wish to turn to more specialised works.

SECTION 1

Principles and process of professional selling

The structure and sequence of the sales process

Before looking at the attitudes, knowledge and skills that are required to become a professional salesperson, it is important to appreciate where selling sits in any commercial environment. Regardless of what is being sold – product or service – the sequence of events is inevitable, although time frames will vary.

There is an indisputable cycle of events in which selling has a key role:

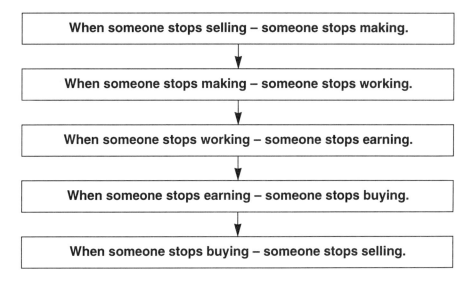

When someone stops selling – someone stops making.

When someone stops making – someone stops working.

When someone stops working – someone stops earning.

When someone stops earning – someone stops buying.

When someone stops buying – someone stops selling.

Start with the buyer – your customer

When anyone is buying anything they will, consciously or unconsciously, pass through the following thought process:

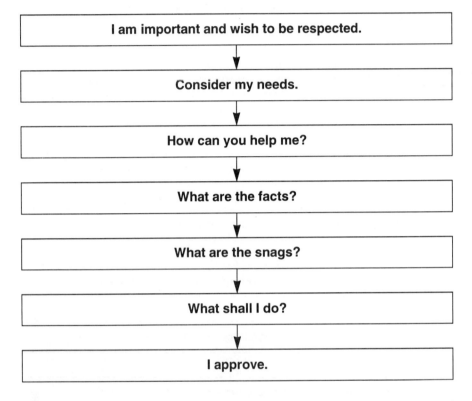

I am important and wish to be respected.

Consider my needs.

How can you help me?

What are the facts?

What are the snags?

What shall I do?

I approve.

Whether it takes a few minutes or several months, the 'buying' mind always goes through this sequence before coming to a decision. It has to be satisfied on each point before it moves to the next point.

The sales sequence

Regardless of what you are selling – product or service, capital goods or consumer products – there is a fundamental sequence of events which needs to happen if you are to satisfy the buyer's needs and conclude the sale.

Time can and will vary from minutes to months, or even years. However, the sequence and process fundamentally remain the same:

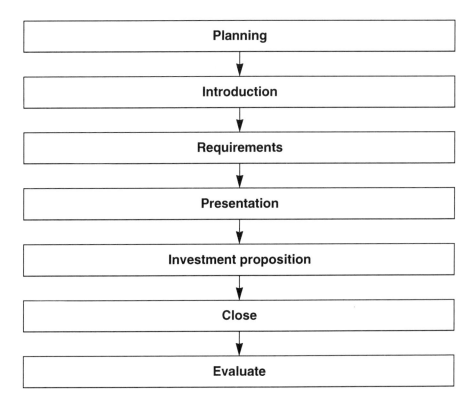

Let us consider each step in the sequence.

Planning

- *What are my objectives for this call?*
- *If an existing customer, what happened on the previous visit?*
- *If a first time contact, what do I know about this company?*
- *What should I know and how can I find out what I do not know?*

- *What objections are likely to arise and have I planned acceptable answers?*
- *Have I all the visual sales aids that may be required?*

Introduction

Remember that you have one chance to make a good first impression. What you say and how you say it will certainly, for a first ever call, have a profound effect on the buyer's attitude.

Your opening statement must be brief, concise, justify the buyer's time and convey confidence and suitable enthusiasm.

On average, this all has to be achieved in no more than 30 seconds.

Requirements

What open questions need to be asked, which will establish or create the relevant needs of this customer?

Presentation

How should the proposition be structured and presented, to show the relevant benefits and advantages to this customer or prospect?

Investment proposition

What is the best way to present the cost and justification? Is it logical? What objections are likely? How can they be countered?

Close/commitment

Related to the call objectives, what commitments are required? What type of close is relevant to this customer? What concessions, if any, could be offered? What would be expected in return?

Evaluate and review

Review the call. Be honest. Ask yourself:

- *To what extent did I achieve all the objectives?*
- *If not, at what point did I lose the initiative?*

- *What needs did I establish or fulfil?*
- *What could I have done differently?*
- *What objectives should I set for the next call?*
- *What lessons have I learnt?*
- *What actions must I now take?*

> **Evaluation of today's failures is the key to tomorrow's success.**

The profile of a professional salesperson

The need to analyse one's own performance and professionalism applies as much to sales personnel as to any person who is committed to self-development. We all have our own strengths and weaknesses. Once this is recognised you are more than half-way there to improving your level of competence.

Before you can evaluate your performance and professionalism as a salesperson, you need to establish:

- what the standards are
- how you will conduct the evaluation
- the process for capitalising on your strengths and resolving your weaknesses
- what help and support you need.

The word 'professionalism' means that a person attains the required standards of performance and maintains them through consistent self-analysis. There is no such thing as an amateur doctor, and salespeople should regard their own profession in a similar light, aiming to achieve a combination of the necessary *attitudes*, *knowledge* and *skills*. To be truly professional, a salesperson should be competent in all three areas. We shall therefore consider attitudes, knowledge and skills in detail.

Attitudes

An attitude is a thought process or state of mind and, to some extent, is likely to be a character trait and, therefore, sometimes difficult to alter. Most people are able to understand the significance and importance of improving certain attitudes and that this leads to increased effectiveness in their work.

Your attitudes influence the way that you are perceived by others; careful analysis is therefore needed, of those attitudes which are necessary to become a professional salesperson.

Positive

Positive attitudes are healthy and constructive; negative attitudes are unhealthy and destructive. A positive person thinks of how something difficult can be done; a negative person thinks of all the reasons why it cannot be done.

Belief in selling

Manufacturing processes are being changed and improved continually and accountancy and administration have been revolutionised by the computer; yet no better method for marketing goods and services has been found than professional selling ability.

Enthusiasm

Enthusiasm is infectious. In a child enthusiasm often makes it difficult for a parent to say 'no', and the same applies to a salesperson/buyer relationship. An enthusiastic salesperson will be able to succeed in spite of limited product knowledge and other obstacles that may arise.

Determination

Many people start off well but finish badly because they lack the determination required to overcome the difficulties they will almost always meet in the course of achieving their objectives.

Appearance

Without knowing it, a salesperson is judged for 'acceptability' within a few minutes of meeting a new contact. First impressions are important and appearance, friendliness, and alertness are just some of the factors which contribute to this impression. **You only get one chance to make a good first impression.**

Initiative

A salesperson needs to be an initiator and to be self-motivated.

Reliable

This is an excellent example to use as a means of assessing whether a person has good or bad attitudes. In general, unreliable people convey bad attitudes which are not conducive to good commercial relationships.

Of course, the above list of attitudes is by no means comprehensive; such things as integrity, confidence, a sense of humour and a capacity for hard work are all relevant. Self-analysis is very much an attitude of mind, and individuals should practise this to identify other attitudes which may need developing, or which are even missing.

Knowledge

Knowledge is power. The following list is by no means exhaustive.

Product and product application knowledge

Complete understanding of the company's product range, its applications and, in particular, how 'product features' can be presented as 'buyer benefits'.

Company knowledge

Company background, policies, departments and procedures. Company personnel and what they do.

Competitor knowledge

Knowledge of competitor activity and market tactics, their products, features, prices, special offers, discounting structures, etc.

Territory knowledge

Knowledge of existing and potential outlets for the company's products. Territory geography and local conditions.

Sales goals and targets/responsibilities

A clear understanding of all sales goals and targets. Levels of responsibility and company's expectations are fully understood.

Skills

The skills required to maintain good attitudes and high levels of knowledge. The main skills may be listed as follows:

- Self-management: setting objectives, planning their attainment and monitoring progress towards this.
- Territory planning to exploit its full potential.
- Communicative skills: asking the right questions, listening, really hearing.
- Presenting benefits that fulfil customer needs.
- Using visual aids and carrying out demonstrations.
- Closing sales with 'action decisions'.
- Overcoming objections.
- Making the most effective use of time.

Actions to develop own performance

On the job training and coaching by your manager or skilled field trainer is the most effective and complete way to develop your skills as a salesperson.

Discuss this with your manager and agree a field training schedule.

Activity 1

Prepare your own profile

Prepare a list of the attitudes, knowledge and skills that you believe are necessary to become a professional salesperson in your industry. You may find the table overleaf helpful.

ATTITUDE, KNOWLEDGE AND SKILLS PROFILE

Attitudes	Knowledge	Skills

Activity 2

Analyse your own strengths and weaknesses

- Having completed your own profile in conjunction with your manager, complete a strengths and weaknesses self-analysis. You may find the table overleaf helpful.

- Prepare an action plan to capitalise on your strengths and action to correct the weaknesses.

- Agree time frames.

STRENGTHS AND WEAKNESSES SELF-ANALYSIS

Strengths	Weaknesses

Activity 3

Fifteen important principles of selling – self-analysis

The self-analysis checklist overleaf gives you the opportunity to assess yourself against fifteen important principles of selling. In the final analysis you are the key to your own development and future success.

Having conducted the self-analysis, prepare a detailed action plan to resolve the weaknesses and how you can capitalise on the strengths.

How to score

Score yourself on a forced rating scale, that is, avoid any reference to average as this would become a meaningless exercise. Who is average?

- 8 Consistently good.
- 6 Training for improvement only.
- 4 Some training needed.
- 2 Much training needed.

Note: There is little merit in totalling all the figures, as it is the level of competence in each principle that is the key consideration.

THE FIFTEEN IMPORTANT PRINCIPLES OF SELLING CHECKLIST

1 Enthusiasm   *Personal score*
Do you:
- convey it through your body language, smile, eyes, voice, posture?   _____
- convey it, regardless of personal feelings?   _____

2 Positiveness
Do you:
- think positively?   _____
- act decisively?   _____
- speak confidently – avoid negative words and phrases?   _____

3 Right mental attitudes
Do you:
- have the strength of your convictions?   _____
- have positive attitudes towards others?   _____
- have positive attitudes towards your company?   _____
- identify negative thoughts for what they really are?   _____

4 Appearance
Do you:
- project the image which is appropriate to the situation? _____

5 Asking questions
Do you:
- stimulate discussion by asking open questions?   _____
- understand the difference between 'open' and 'closed' questions?   _____
- make effective use of 'open' and 'closed' questions at the appropriate times?   _____

6 Managing your time

Do you:

- plan your work and work your plan? _____
- analyse the way you spend your time? _____
- seek to maximise your sales activity? _____

7 Verbal communication

Do you:

- communicate precisely and clearly? _____
- use appropriate language? _____
- avoid slang or jargon? _____

8 Visual sales aids

Do you:

- use appropriate visual sales aids to illustrate effectively what you are saying? _____
- understand the use and range of available visual sales aids? _____

9 Listening

Do you:

- listen for buying signals? _____
- listen to what the customer is saying and really hear? _____

10 Sales objections

Do you:

- understand what causes a sales objection? _____
- know how and when to deal with sales objections? _____
- anticipate and attempt to pre-empt sales objections? _____

11 Features and benefits

Do you:

- know the difference between features and benefits? _____
- sell what your product will do? _____
- relate benefits to customer needs? _____

Continued overleaf

12 Persistence

Do you:

- understand the importance of asking for the order more than once? _____
- see a refusal as an opportunity rather than a rejection? _____

13 Product knowledge

Do you:

- identify the extent of your product knowledge? _____
- find ways to improve and update your product knowledge? _____
- know all the features and benefits of all your products? _____
- have available all the visual sales aids relating to your products? _____

14 Self-development

Do you:

- see the personal benefit of self-development? _____
- assess your own strengths and weaknesses? _____
- consider yourself to be receptive to new ideas and techniques? _____
- evaluate the benefits of new ideas and techniques? _____
- plan how you can capitalise on your strengths? _____
- plan what you can do to correct the weaknesses? _____

15 Sales development

Do you:

- analyse the results of your area? _____
- identify opportunities for new business? _____
- analyse your activity levels? _____
- identify who are your major accounts? _____
- have a development plan for your area? _____

SECTION 2

The skills of professional selling and negotiation

Effective communications

Communication – effective two-way communication in all mediums – is the stock-in-trade of a professional salesperson. However, all too often poor communication, or the lack of it, is singled out as the cause of mistrust, misunderstanding and sometimes aggression and consequently lost business.

There are fundamentally three key ways in which to communicate. Verbal and written are the most obvious but body language also plays a significant part. Effective and good communicators have one thing in common, they plan. Personal factors can and often do play a significant part in communication. Here is a list of some individual differences that need to be considered.

Age	The 'generation gap' leading to different interests, values, experiences, needs, language.
Appearance	Unusual physical features or modes of dress may either inhibit or foster communications.
Background	Social upbringing which gives different values and expectations.
Education	Different levels give vast ranges of vocabulary and concepts.
Health	Hearing, sight, resistance to stress, level of adjustment.
Intelligence	Mental agility, types of concepts found easy/difficult to understand and manipulate.
Interests	Social, practical, intellectual, domestic.
Language	Verbal agility, type of 'jargon' used.
Personality	Energy, stability, sociability, withdrawn, tough, tender, secure, insecure, assertive, passive, etc.
Race	Cultural differences and communicative etiquettes.
Religion	Influencing culture and beliefs.
Sex	The ease or difficulty of communicating with people of the opposite sex.
Training	Level of skill, occupational specialism, technical knowledge.

The principles of persuasive communications

What do we mean by communication?

In simple terms, we mean the transfer of an identical message from one person to another.

But to the salesperson, whose living depends upon success in communicating persuasively, communicating means more than this. The objectives are to make the listener not only

understand and *agree* but also *act;*

and in order to ensure that they are progressively achieving these objectives, they must also achieve *feedback*.

What are the main obstructions to successful communication?

The first problem is to recognise that despite what many people believe, communicating successfully is not easy.

The second problem is to accept that the onus is on the communicator to achieve successful communication and not on the receiver.

Communication planning

In all communications the following factors need to be carefully considered:

Aim	What is the communication aiming to achieve? What do you want to happen as a result of the communication?
Communicator	What is the relationship between the sender and the recipient? Have you all the relevant facts? Are there relevant time frames?
Methods	What is the best communication method to use. Do you need to telephone and confirm in writing?

Situation	In what situation will the communication be received? Where and to whom should it be sent? Should it be 'Private and Confidential'?
Recipient	What is the recipient expecting? Have you made it clear what action you expect?
Content	Is the message clear and logical? Have you communicated all that you intended? Have you avoided or minimised any assumptions?

Eliminate negative questions, statements or phrases

Use decisive and specific words. Avoid indecisive words and phrases, such as:

'More or less'	*'In a manner of speaking'*
'Roughly'	*'Thereabouts'*
'Approximately'	*'It would be fair to say'*
'Almost'	*'Etcetera'*
'Possibly'	*'Nearly'*
'May be'	*'About'*
'Likely'	*'Sort of/kind of'*

Avoid the 'ers' and 'ums'

Think carefully, speak slowly, use a steady voice, and pause to allow the listener time to consider what you have said.

If you do not speak fluently and use 'ers' and 'ums', the listener will gain the impression that you are unsure of your facts.

Do not use clichés

Except in extreme cases, the use of clichés represents habit and poor word and phrase selection. Remember that a buyer who sees several salespeople a day will have heard these hundreds of times, and will be more interested in how often you use clichés than in your sales presentation.

Typical examples are:

'Fair enough'	*'Let's face it'*
'In this day and age'	*'At this point in time'*
'Speaking frankly'	*'In my considered opinion'*
'You know'	*'No way'*
'Where I am coming from'	*'At the end of the day'*

Use a person's name

Know who you are speaking to and use their names. If you do not know them, ask and remember them, as nothing is as sweet to an individual, as his or her own name.

Avoid familiar terms of address

Remember that you are a business person, there to conduct business. It is unprofessional and may give offence, if such terms as 'Dear' or 'Love' are used when addressing people.

Never assume

Assuming that people understand what you are saying is folly.

To **assume** makes an **ass** of **you** and **me**.

A picture is worth a thousand words

Support your communication wherever possible with graphic examples. One famous experiment showed that in verbal communication only, people forget

29% in 1 hour
90% in 3 days

With supporting visual aids, the memory loss is dramatically reduced to only

14% in 1 hour
35% in 3 days

Analysis of memory retention/loss using verbal or visual communication methods, or both

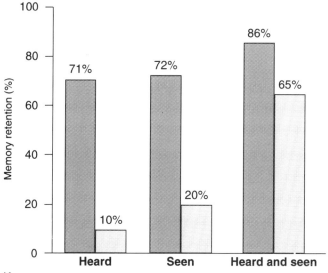

Key:

▓ Remembered after 1 hour

☐ Remembered after 3 days

The right voice

The tone, speed, clarity and loudness of the voice may convey aggression, uncertainty, boredom or even unconscious insolence. Progress and customer confidence can be significantly restricted through the tone of your voice. Enthusiasm is fine if controlled and measured. Too much can be overbearing and convey pressure.

Effective listening

This is not a skill that comes easily to many, including many salespeople. If you talk, you are saying only what you already know. If you listen, you may learn something you did not know before. The salesperson who does all the talking and little listening is often perceived to be adopting high pressure tactics. People are resistant to this type of approach because of the fear that they are being 'sold to'. On the other hand they may be quite happy to 'buy' because of the implication that the decision is in their own hands.

As already discussed, asking questions is a vital skill for any professional salesperson or for all wishing to improve their communication skills. There is no point, however, in asking questions if you do not listen to the answers. Being able to present solutions based on what you have heard is often very simple if you heard what has been said.

Almost everyone can improve their listening skills. Compare yourself against the key principles of effective listening and take appropriate steps to improve where you find a deficiency. You may be surprised at the personal benefits achieved. The following comment says it all.

'The less you talk the more you hear
. . . and consequently learn.'

Listening skills

L   Look interested
- Face the speaker.
- Keep eye contact.
- Stay relaxed.
- Lean forward slightly.
- Maintain an open posture.

I   Inquire with questions
- Clarify the speaker's meaning.
- Ensure you get the full story.
- Use open questions.

S   Stick to the point
- Remember your purpose.
- Listen for the central theme.
- Wait for the complete message – don't prejudge.
- Don't say 'yes, but . . .'. Be patient – don't interrupt.

T   Test your understanding
- Ensure you really understand what is being said.
- Restate to make sure – 'So what you are really saying is . . .'

E **Evaluate the message**

- Identify the speaker's purpose.
- Analyse what is being said.
- *Reasoning*: flaws or fallacies, generalisations, causes linked to effects, emotional appeal.
- *Evidence*: facts or assumptions, complete or partial, information source, up to date, reliable.
- *Language*: familiar word, jargon, body language consistent with the verbal message.
- *Voice*: tone, pitch, speed of delivery.

N **Neutralise your feelings**

- Stay calm, retain self control.
- Don't get heated or emotional.
- Keep an open mind.

You hear with the ears – but listen with the mind.

Body language

We all communicate with our bodies at least as much as we do with our mouths. Reading and understanding this aspect of communication is a helpful skill. If the body language and the spoken word appear to contradict each other, believe the body language.

Although it is a specialised subject, we all to some degree read body language instinctively and, as with all aspects of communication, some more effectively than others.

The most potent organ of body language is the face, particularly the eyes. By keeping good eye contact with the customer, we can check whether the expressions of the face and eyes reinforce what is being said (or not said). The face and eyes will convey interest or boredom, belief or suspicion, liking or distaste, far more quickly and clearly than the spoken word. The stance of the whole body will help to show whether the customer is relaxed or tense, impatient and wanting to move off or content to stay.

Mannerisms can indicate that an individual is loosing interest in the conversation and not listening. Such mannerisms in salespeople are both rude and irritating. Examples are:

- finger tapping
- doodling
- fidgeting
- chair tilting
- gazing
- hair smoothing
- face touching.

Restrict your movements to those necessary to put over your sales message. Use questions where relevant, but avoid excesses.

Remember. *You have two eyes, two ears and one mouth.* Use them in that proportion and you will improve your skills of communication.

Written communications

Good written communication conveys the idea or message to the reader with maximum clarity in the minimum number of words.

The ten key principles of written communication

1 Write directly to the point.

2 Use simple words that should be familiar to the reader.

3 Keep your sentences short.

4 Avoid 'padding'. Quality is more important than quantity.

5 Plan your writing to have a beginning, middle and end.

6 Use 'you will see' rather than 'it will be noticed'.

7 Avoid clichés and catch-phrases.

8 Write to appeal to the receiver's intellect.

9 Check and read before sending.

10 Remember the difference between *informing* and *performing*.

Pitfalls to avoid in written communication

1 Do not use jargon.

2 Too few words can cause the meaning to become lost or ambiguous.

3 Too many words can have the same effect.

4 Illegible writing does not help the reader, or the typist.

BUSINESS LETTERS – CHECKLIST

- Is the aim clear?

- Who will read the letter?

- Is the letter directed towards that person?

- Is the opening a preamble or does it create interest?

- Have the facts been verified?

- Has it been checked for long complex sentences?

- Is it grammatically correct?

- Does it punch home vital words?

- Does it stress benefits?

- Have as many 'I's as possible been cut out?

- Is it free of any hackneyed phrases?

- Does it create confidence?

- Does it create desire?

- Does it show understanding of the reader's problems?

- Are superlatives overused?

- Is it the kind of letter that *you* would like to receive?

- Is it positive? (Not 'Please do not hesitate').

- Does it inform the reader what you want them to do?

- Is the receiver clear about what you will do next?

- Have you avoided 'urgent' and 'as soon as possible' but quantified time frames?

- Does it fully meet the expectations of the receiver?

- Have you checked the receiver's name, initials, title and spelling?

Call planning and preparation

> To fail to prepare is to prepare to fail.

An old adage but it has a ring of truth. Too many people, including managers and salespeople, fail to give sufficient time to planning for some inexplicable reason. They give all the excuses, one of which is lack of time. Time is a manageable commodity and the lack of it is often caused by a lack of genuine commitment to planning.

Remember successful salespeople do the things that unsuccessful salespeople do not like doing, and planning is often top of the list.

It is claimed that detailed planning is 60 per cent of any successful call. It generates quiet confidence and it shows that you are a professional person who is ready to conduct business, rather than a self-centred slick-talking individual.

You need a pad, pencil, customer record card, any relevant company initiatives or promotions and some quiet thinking time. Many salespeople will use a pre-printed sales planning sheet: an example is given on page 32.

Total reliance on memory and experience can let you down and does not promote customer confidence in you and your company. Ask yourself the following questions and make notes where relevant.

Where am I going?

If you don't know where you are going, you cannot plan an economical route and time will be wasted. Plan your journey to maximise selling time. Selling time is too valuable to waste on unnecessary travelling. Considering all the alternatives could well give you the time to make that extra call.

Why am I calling?

If the answer to this is a courtesy call, don't bother. Such reasons are a waste of time and will often only serve to annoy the customer and discredit yourself. There must be a sound objective for every call both

CALL PLAN
Customer name:
Contact:
Date and time:
Date of last call:
Call objectives:
Points to discuss:
Actions agreed/comments:

qualitative and quantitative. Wherever possible, there must be at least three objectives for each call, one primary and two secondary.

With careful customer records, call objectives can be identified from previous notes. Objectives for a prospect call could well be to gain key information to aid subsequent calls.

Who am I going to see?

For existing customers, your customer records should provide most of this information and answer the question 'What happened when I last called?' When dealing with large companies, the buying decision may well be influenced by many departments. Be aware of who they are and how and when they need to be contacted. For new customers it is a question of checking who is the decision-maker but also who are the people (influences) who may be involved.

What else do I need to consider?

- *What is the nature of this business?*
- *What are their present or potential needs?*
- *What competition am I up against?*
- *Is their business expanding or contracting?*
- *Am I gaining an increased share of their business?*
- *Do I need to confirm?*
- *Do I know where to go and how to get there?*
- *How long will the journey take?*

How should I conduct the call?

- *What tactics should be used?*
- *What concession, if any, should/could be offered?*
- *What samples do I need?*
- *What visual sales aids do I need?*
- *What objections may arise and do I have the answers?*
- *Should I anticipate these objections in the presentation?*

Typical sales call objectives

- To obtain an order/specification.
- To follow-up a quotation/enquiry with a view to closing the deal.
- To gain acceptance of a sample for test.
- To gain agreement to visit branches.
- To gain agreement to visit end users.
- To introduce technical personnel.
- To carry out a feasibility study.
- To obtain market intelligence (breakdown).
- To gain introductions to other contacts within a company.
- To sell other products in the range.
- To obtain a demonstration.
- To check stocks.
- To discuss drawings/data.
- To leave samples.
- To settle a complaint.
- To review service levels/standards.
- To discuss future needs/support.
- To review business to date.

Activity 4

Establishing call objectives for existing and potential customers

List all the typical call objectives possible for your product/service for:

1   Existing customers

_____

_____

_____

_____

_____

_____

_____

_____

2   Potential customers

_____

_____

_____

_____

_____

_____

_____

Establishing customer needs

Questioning technique

The essence of successful selling can be expressed in one simple equation:

> **Fulfil customer's needs = Sale**

The key to establishing customer needs brings into play two of the most important skills in the salesperson's tool box:

- **Asking questions.** Ask the right type of questions.
- **Listening.** Really listen to the answers.

Two qualities which may also have a direct bearing on how you are perceived commercially and socially are: are you a boring person to talk to, or an interesting person asking interesting questions?

Clearly there are many key skills to master in becoming a successful salesperson. However, understanding the role and significance of questioning and which questions to use is one of the most important.

Two basic types of question play an important part in the sales process.

- **Closed questions** are used to check facts, summarise. The response has to be yes or no. Closed questions have a key role to play in closing the sale or gaining commitment – a theme which we shall return to in the section on closing.
- **Open questions** invite dialogue. Why 'open'? Questions asked in such a way, prefaced with any of the following seven words, will normally provoke an extended and usually informative answer:
  - *What?*
  - *Why?*
  - *When?*
  - *How?*
  - *Where?*
  - *Who?*
  - *Which?*

Add the phrases 'To what extent?' 'In what circumstances?' and 'What value ...?', and you have ten powerful ways to develop a conversation, gain information and begin to establish the customer's needs.

There is one word in the questioning technique, 'Why?', that needs to be considered separately. Firstly, if you ask why as the first question on a subject, it can sound like interrogation which may antagonise the listener. Secondly, it is a perfect supplementary question after a response, to follow up with 'That is interesting. Why do you say that?' or 'Why is that?'

For example: 'Mr Morgan, what type of ... do you currently prefer?' Listen to his reply, then respond with 'I see. Why is that?' The 'Why?' question will invariably reveal his opinion.

Open questions also serve another very important function. They raise the level of rapport between the sales person and customer for two reasons:

- You are seen as someone who is interested in the customer and what the customer wants.
- People like to talk and will warm to those who ask interesting questions.

Open and closed questions also play a key part in dealing with and overcoming objections, because until you know all the facts and what is behind the objection, you are shooting in the dark.

Rudyard Kipling was a journalist before he became an author. He recognised the power and value of open questions in obtaining information and composed the following rhyme:

> *I keep six honest serving-men*
> *(They taught me all I knew)*
> *Their names are WHAT and WHY and WHEN*
> *And HOW and WHERE and WHO.*

Planning

For some reason many people will naturally ask closed questions and find great difficulty in using open questions. It therefore needs consistent practice and planning.

Before making each call consider the call objectives and what information you need to obtain and write down all the open questions you need to ask. This is particularly important when calling on prospective customers.

- *If you do not ask, how will you know?*
- *If you do not know, how can you sell?*

Having asked questions, listen and be seen to listen to the answer, taking detailed notes where possible. This not only conveys genuine interest, but enables you to play back the key points using the customer's own words when presenting your proposals.

Listening

> **When we talk we teach, when we listen we learn.**

- Limit your conversation.
- Record 'key' words.
- Do not interrupt.
- Be patient.
- Shut out distractions.
- Regularly confirm information.
- Listen actively – 'Yes' 'I See' 'Oh really'.

Activity 5

Planning questions to ask existing and potential customers

Using the information in the section on call planning, write down all the open questions that you need to ask to obtain the relevant information. You can use the forms provided on the following pages.

WHAT QUESTIONS NEED TO BE ASKED?

Existing customer

1	
2	
3	
4	
5	
6	
7	
8	
9	
10	
11	
12	
13	
14	
15	
16	
17	
18	
19	
20	

WHAT QUESTIONS NEED TO BE ASKED?

Potential customer

1	
2	
3	
4	
5	
6	
7	
8	
9	
10	
11	
12	
13	
14	
15	
16	
17	
18	
19	
20	

Features and benefits

What do people buy – what are you selling?

To the question 'Do you need to have a good knowledge of your company and its products?' without hesitation the answer would be 'yes'.

Product and service knowledge

Product knowledge can mean different things to different people. To some, product knowledge is concerned only with what the company has put into the product, together with all the detailed technical specifications. Complete product knowledge means knowing not only what it is, but even more important, what it will do.

Most companies, large or small, will claim that they have a wide range of technical and specialist support together with after-sales support, or will make guarantee claims. But what does that mean? What is good service? What does guarantee mean? What is after-sales support?

This is like asking 'How long is a piece of string?'

- What does the customer expect from good service?
- What does the customer expect from a guarantee?
- What does the customer expect from the after-sales service?

When discussing the buying process, you will recall that the first two stages for the customer are:

1 I am important and wish to be respected.

2 Consider my needs.

Unless you meet those needs to the customer's satisfaction, the likelihood of a successful sale is minimal. This applies to everyone involved in selling, irrespective of product or service. Remember there are few monopolies in the world. Most products and services are subject to alternative sources of supply.

It is important to establish that price is not the sole key to a successful sale. Consequently, the professional will avoid using the word 'cheapest' as it conveys inferior product. Remember that 'you get what you pay for', 'value for money' and 'competitive price' have a better sound.

$$\boxed{\text{Benefits} \times \text{Price} = \text{Successful sale}}$$

People buy what the product can do so know what your customer wants done.

What are features?

Features are the terms used to describe a product. They are often tangible, reflecting design, research, appearance, specification and components. They can also be non-tangible, for example, back-up services, company history, financial standing.

They may sound good to you but what do they mean to the customer?

People do not buy features – they buy benefits.

Benefits

Benefits come from and are a result of a product feature. They are usually intangible but will be experienced through use. When benefits are related to features, customers begin to see a much clearer justification as to why they should commit themselves to your product.

This equally applies when describing all your support areas (features) that your company offers. What does that mean to the customer?

- Claiming that you have excellent back-up service is not enough. What kind of back-up service?
- Your product is guaranteed. What does the guarantee do?
- Marketing support. What kind of marketing support?

For example:

Feature	Benefit
This watch is fully guaranteed.	If the watch ceases to function correctly, it will be repaired or replaced totally free of charge.
Full marketing support.	You will receive individual support in promoting these products through each of your outlets.

There is often a situation where a technical question requires a technical answer, but again do not always assume that this will be fully understood without explaining the benefits.

When discussing pertinent features and resulting benefits use link phrases such as '... which means that ...' or '... which gives you ...'.

Most companies and their products will have many features with subsequent benefits. However, relating all these parrot fashion will only serve to confuse and is likely to foster indecision. Only present those features and benefits that you have identified through questioning as being relevant.

There are two further factors which are involved when people buy: rational and emotional needs. These are often reflected by the mnemonic ENSCADE.

- **Efficiency** – effectiveness, performance.
- **Novelty** – unique, new, outstanding characteristics.
- **Safety** – safe in buying from the company, safe equipment.
- **Convenience** – facilities, comfort, ease.
- **Appearance** – design appeal.
- **Durability** – reliable, lasting.
- **Economy** – investment, profit savings.

While all may have some varying degree of relevance, one or more will be dominant. Identify these and this is where you place the greatest emphasis in terms of benefits. With a customer who likes to be involved in something new, you will focus on novelty. However, with the more cautious customer, you will emphasise the safety and durability points.

Examples of features and benefits incorporating rational and emotional needs

Industrial selling

Feature   The drive shaft of the machine has been made thicker. The shaft will not fail due to overload because it has been designed to take far greater loading stress without distortion.

Major benefits

- *Durability*   Because the shaft has been designed in this way, it will have longer life.

- *Economy*   Because of the stronger shaft, its running life is greater and you will therefore obtain greater productivity from your investment.

- *Novelty*   This is the only machine on the market which gives you the advantage of this stronger, more durable shaft.

Consumer selling

Feature   The product is packaged in a strong box with a cellophane top.

Major benefits

- *Convenience*   The uniform design of the package enables easier storage and handling and stacks will not fall over.

- *Safety*   The strong package design means there is no fear of the product being crushed in storage or handling.

- *Appearance*   The package is designed to attract the consumer, and to act as a promotional aid.

- *Durability*   The careful design of the package means the product is maintained in good condition, and the packaging is less likely to get damaged.

Activity 6

Identifying the features and benefits of your company and its products

1a List all the features of your products/services.
Write all the benefits/advantages related to each feature.

b List all the features of your company.
Write all the benefits/advantages related to each feature.

You may use the forms provided on the following pages.

c Evaluate your company or product brochure.
Does it sell the benefits?

Remember *each feature can have more than one benefit. Don't forget to state the obvious. If you don't say it, the customer will not hear it.*

2 Using the completed features and benefits lists, relate each benefit to ENSCADE.

Product/service:

Feature		Benefit
	W	
	H	
	I	
	C	
	H	
	M	
	E	
	A	
	N	
	S	
	T	
	H	
	A	
	T	

Remember, you can only relate benefits when you have discovered a need.

Company:

Feature	WHICH MEANS THAT	Benefit
	W	
	H	
	I	
	C	
	H	
	M	
	E	
	A	
	N	
	S	
	T	
	H	
	A	
	T	

Remember, you can only relate benefits when you have discovered a need.

Dealing with and overcoming sales objections

Many salespeople fear sales objections, brush them aside and present their product or service parrot-fashion, perpetuating the image of pressure salespeople claiming that their products or services are the panacea for all problems.

The professional salesperson will welcome objections as a clear signal that there is some genuine interest.

Imagine a situation where there are no objections whatsoever. In most cases you have a real problem – no interest.

Before considering how to handle sales objections, it is important to evaluate first what are the likely causes of many objections and how we can minimise their impact on the sales process.

Likely causes of sale objections

- Presenting badly.
- Blinding people with science.
- Emphasising wrong/irrelevant features and benefits.
- Poor demonstration.
- Inadequate/poor product knowledge.
- Negative salesperson.
- Poor communication.
- Not listening to, or discovering customer's needs.
- Lack of information.
- Talking to the wrong person.

In other words – poor selling.

Identifying the sales objection

It has to be recognised that people will not always tell you the real reason when raising an objection, not necessarily for any devious reasons, but to avoid discussing the real facts. It could also be that at this stage they are not totally comfortable with the salesperson. So clearly one key point to establish in any process is – are we dealing with the real objection?

It is therefore important to classify the objection.

Frivolous objection

Not always easy to recognise. Could be a personal experience, bias, taste. However if you judge it to be frivolous, avoid getting involved. Smile, ignore and press on. If it persists, acknowledge and agree to deal with it later.

Genuine and false objections

Genuine objections may be caused by past experience, resistance to change, or by not being convinced.

False objections may be a smoke screen, for example, stating that the price is too high; or the person may not have the authority to buy.

Real objections will need to be resolved to the customer's satisfaction before a commitment or a sale can be agreed.

When to deal with the objection

The next key issue is when do you deal with the objection, particularly if you are in the middle of your sales presentation and you may well be covering that very point later? You do not want to be side-tracked, which can and often does have a devastating impact on your presentation and can be the prelude to failure.

Acknowledge the objection immediately it is raised, for example:

'That's an interesting point.'
'Glad that you raised that issue.'
'I understand your concern.'

Deal with it then if you wish or acknowledge and say 'I will return to that point later', and be seen where practicable, to write the objection down. This will signal your genuine intent and the customer in the main will feel comfortable that the objection will be resolved at some time and will continue to listen to your presentation.

Fail to acknowledge or brush aside the objection and you will have problems. The customer will feel disturbed, even angry, that the point (however trivial it may seem to you) has not been given the respect and attention it clearly deserves. Without doubt you will rapidly lose the attention of the customer who will seek the first opportunity to dismiss you – which you will deserve.

So far we have:

- recognised the need and established the causes of objections
- recognised the need to acknowledge the objection
- recognised the need to classify the objection
- recognised the need to decide when to deal with the objection.

Now we will consider how to handle the objection, covering all those issues.

How to handle sales objections

There are a number of recognised systems and sequences which can assist you in dealing with a sales objection. Here are two of the most effective and widely used.

The most used is probably **A Q R S C**:

Agree or appear to agree

'I can understand how you feel'.
'That is an understandable point'.

Even if you have the answer do not dismiss and come back with the answer.

Question

Establish the facts. Ask questions.

'Why do you say that'? 'What happened'? 'When was that'?

Re-state

Play back the objection. Show that you understand. Get a 'Yes, that is the problem'.

> *'I understand that what you are saying is that you need to be reassured on the . . .'*
> *'You would be interested if we could convince you of the . . .'*

If the response is 'No', you are likely to be facing a false objection.

> *'Oh! I see M . . . . What exactly is the problem?'*

The real objection could well surface. There is little point in continuing the attempt to answer the problem if the customer is not prepared to consider the answer.

Continue to ask polite but searching open questions.

Satisfy

Now explain all the reasons why, using relevant benefits, visual aids, third party testimony, etc. to support your reasons.

Close

Close on a commitment to go ahead now that objection is resolved and continue your sales presentation. Now you want a 'Yes'.

> *'Does that answer your query?'*
> *'Has that clarified things for you?'*

Remember: **A Q R S C**

A second useful system is the **five step approach**:

Step 1: Listen

Really 'hear' what the customer is saying.

Step 2: Cushion/Agree

Acknowledge what the customer is saying. Do not directly respond to the objection. It could raise fear or even aggression.

Step 3: Condition

Condition the customer mind to consider logical evidence, without losing face. People do not like to be proved wrong and lose face. Consider the objection as a question. What is being asked? It may well be that he or she is anticipating objections that may be raised at some time in the future by their customers.

Step 4: Key evidence

Present the key evidence.

Step 5: Action

Ask for the order/commitment.

Closer examination of this process will identify some *key* phrases to complement the five steps.

- **Steps 1 & 2:** Reassure. Do not resent the objection. The key is to explain and guide.
  'I appreciate your concern.'
  'I can understand the point that you raise.'
  'You have raised a good point.'

- **Step 3:** Convert the objection into a question.
  'The question in your mind, M ..., is are the additional features and benefits worth the higher price?'
  If he or she says *'No'*, then clearly there is a deeper point.
  Ask *'I see. What precisely is the question/concern?'*
  Listen to the response and respond.

- **Step 4:** Present your response using all available evidence, for example, visual aids, third party testimony.

- **Step 5:** Gain acceptance/commitment and where relevant close on the order.

Many salespeople are defeated before they start. They fail to recognise that objections are to be welcomed and can often be a buying signal (a point to be discussed in the section on closing) and the key to the order. They may convince themselves that the problem lies with their product or service.

- As long as a prospect continues to object, they are *still* a potential customer.
- So do not let sales objections become the locked door.
- Search for the key – it is there if you look and listen.

Activity 7

Developing positive techniques for dealing with sales objections

1 List the sales objections you encounter most.

_____

_____

_____

_____

_____

_____

2 Develop strong, positive answers to each sales objection.

_____

_____

_____

_____

_____

_____

3 Convert your six most frequent sales objections into the form of questions that can be used in the conditioning phase.

_____

_____

_____

_____

_____

_____

_____

4 Evaluate and consider, how the most common sales objections can be pre-handled in your sales presentation.

_____

_____

_____

_____

_____

_____

_____

Closing

This is the moment of truth, the point at which you ask the person or persons to whom you are selling a product or service to make a decision, 'yes' or 'no', or a commitment to continue. In principle it is the last step in the sales process, but in fact the right time to close can arrive at any stage in the sales interview.

It is a proven fact that this is where most sales agreements are lost, through three fundamental mistakes:

1 Simply not asking.

2 Not asking at the right time.

3 Accepting the first 'no' as final.

In considering the skill, and what a vital skill, one needs to understand:

- what closing is
- why you should close
- when to close
- who should close
- which close to use
- how many times you should close.

What is closing?

A close is any question that you ask where the answer confirms that the recipient agrees or not to buy or give commitment to action in the buying process. In many sales situations, capital contracts or major investments, the whole sales process can span many meetings covering months or even years. However, at each meeting some form of commitment will be established. So remember, closing is not just asking for the order, but asking for a commitment.

To close a sale you must ask a closing question.

Why and who should close?

Not such a silly question as it sounds. As a salesperson, you are the person who should ask for the decision. Rarely if ever will the customers close for you, although they may give certain indications that they are interested and want you to close. Only too often, salespeople do not close the sale because they are afraid they might receive a 'no', but failing to recognise that they might get a 'yes'.

Remember, you cannot lose what you have not got. However, is a 'no' such a terrible thing? Not to the professional. Failing to close is in essence asking the buyer to ask to be allowed to buy! The reason for this is usually that the salesperson is afraid to risk having his/her pride injured by being rejected.

A 'no' response will usually mean 'I want more information, you have not totally fulfilled my needs'.

After every sales call ask yourself the key question: *Did I actually ask?*

When to close

From the moment that you start planning the call you are in fact starting the closing process. The key to when to close is all about listening – really hearing what the customer is saying. Often the customer will unconsciously put out buying signals – verbal or non-verbal indications that they are interested in making a decision.

Examples of verbal signals

- *'It seems pretty good to me.'*
- *'When could I get delivery?'*
- *'I can't see anything wrong with it.'*
- *'Do you make it in other sizes/colours?'*
- *'What are your payment terms?'*

Examples of non-verbal body language signals

- Picking up the product.
- Picking up the proposal/quotation.

- Making a positive gesture – moving forward or backward in the chair.
- Nodding the head in approval/facial expression.
- Giving a knowing and positive gesture to a colleague.

See or hear one of these and this is the point to draw quickly to a conclusion what you are saying, forget everything else that you were going to say and **ask for the order/commitment**.

Failure to hear this buying signal, keep on talking and you are more than likely going to talk yourself right out of the other side – and out of an order. You are likely to hear those immortal words: *'I need time to think it over.'*

The closing question

To close a sale or gain commitment to the next phase, you must ask a closing question. Whenever you ask a closing question, shut up. Keep quiet and wait.

Use the power of silence – do not interrupt the customer's thinking. To do so will be fatal. This is the point when many sales are lost because salespeople cannot control their mouths. It may seem like an eternity, but wait for the customer to speak first.

If you have closed at the right time, the answer is likely to be 'yes' or a small point clarification and then a 'yes'.

If it is 'no', it is no major problem. Find out what the doubt is, and then move into another closing situation. **Close sooner rather than later.**

> **Samson killed ten thousand Philistines with the jaw bone of an ass.**
>
> **Twenty thousand sales are killed every day with the same weapon.**

Which close to use

There are at least ten different ways and variations in which to close a sale or gain commitments. There is no set rule in deciding which one to use. Many factors will influence your choice: the personality and character of the customer, the type and environment, also yourself. You will feel more comfortable with some closes than with others.

Listed below are some of the most used types of closes, with suggestions as to which type of situation they are best suited.

Alternative close

This is probably the most widely used close of them all in most situations and the most natural. When you reach the point where you feel the prospects are 'warm' to your product or service, ask them a question with two alternatives. For example,

> 'Will you be taking **four** cases or **two**?'
> 'Would you prefer the **model A or B**?'
> 'Would you like them **this week** or **next week**?'

Do not ask the customer to decide whether to buy, only to choose which size, type, colour or quantity they want to buy.

Objection close

You will recall when discussing ways of dealing with objections, that objections are often the immediate prelude to a sale. Follow the **A Q R S C** system and when re-stating the objection:

> 'If I can convince you about the delivery . . .'
> 'If I can show you that it will fully meet your needs . . .'
> 'If I can convince you that it represents value for money . . .'
>
> '. . . we can go ahead then?'

Fear close

Fear is a human reaction that in certain circumstances plays a part in the closing process, for example, if the customer fears limited supplies or a pending price increase.

Used constructively, in some instances fear closes can be very effective.

Assumptive close

This is another widely used 'natural close'. You assume that the customer is going to place an order, or move on the next phase, and ask a question about the product when it is in their possession such as,

'Where will you site it?'
'When shall we deliver it?'
'When can we start staff training?'

This is a useful close for the indecisive buyer.

Sharp angle close

Often used where you are dealing with an assertive individual, who likes making decisions. When you are asked a direct question, for example,

'Can you supply this in one month?'
'Does it do this?'
'Can you offer an installation package?'

You respond *'Do you want it if we can?'*

The ask for it close

Probably the least used close of all, because the salesperson fears hearing the word 'No'. As long as you have made a professional sales presentation, fulfilled all the customers' needs, it is simply the next logical step. Even if the customers refuse they will raise the objection which gives you the opportunity to convince them. This should be the most frequently used close.

The summary of benefits close

During the presentation, the customer may have forgotten some of the benefits you mentioned, so summarise them. The best way of doing this is to summarise all the benefits in which they have expressed an interest, showing how your product or service can fully meet each need. Gain acknowledgement at each stage.

This is also invaluable if the customer has been distracted, called away, telephoned, etc., at this critical stage in the sales sequence. It is important to refocus the buyer's mind away from the distraction. Fail to do this and the buyer may well cut short the meeting to deal with another issue.

Concession close

Used more in the negotiating arena, this can be a powerful way to clinch a deal. Some salespeople, although this could be considered sharp practice, will build a concession provision into a proposal. In many selling situations, human nature is such that customers like to feel that they have wrung some concession out of a salesperson. This can be powerful, but needs to be used with caution. Concede too much too soon and you will lose credibility and the sale.

Take a tip out of the negotiator's tool box – never concede anything without gaining a concession. This will avoid the concession spiral.

Trial close

This can be used quite early in the sales sequence, where you are getting very positive responses and questions. Use to test the water and it may well get a positive response or certainly draw out pending objections.

'I will think it over'

This is one of the most common objections that you will have to overcome. The problem is that you may not be certain what the real objection is. What you must do is identify the objection. For example:

Customer: *'I'll think it over.'*

Salesperson: *'That's fine. I understand that you need to give this very careful thought.* (empathy). *In order that you have all the facts, which point is it that you wish to consider?'*

Then you can move into an objection or summary close.

How many times should you close?

In this competitive climate, customers, buyers or whoever is making a purchasing decision, need to be totally convinced and reassured that the decision is the right one. When they say 'no' it invariably means 'You have not convinced me'. The salesperson's role is to identify and resolve this doubt.

Successful sales are completed every day by salespeople who close sales long after they have heard the first, second and third 'no'. These salespeople have the courage and confidence to ask for the order again and again because they do not take 'no' as a personal rejection. Many expert salespeople will tell you that fewer than three closes and you have not tried.

The general of a victorious army once praised the perseverance of his men by saying *'Our soldiers are not any braver than those of the enemy, they are just brave for five minutes longer'*.

Conclusion

If the decision is not to be made at this interview, or if indeed the customer wants time to consider, close on a commitment:

'When will you make the decision?'

'When can I come back to you?'

'When can I call to discuss this further?'

Remember: after the call ask yourself – did I actually close?

Activity 8

Analysing your closing techniques

1 Think of the last six times that you were successful. What type of close did you use?

2 Think of the last six times that you were unsuccessful, and ask yourself:

   ● Were there any buying signals?

   ● Did you close at the right time?

   ● Did you close?

   ● How could you have handled it differently?

Sales negotiation

The market in which we compete with other companies has three characteristics:

1 Similarity of products/services.

2 Similarity in prices/discounts/terms.

3 The presentation to the customer.

The latter is where one company can be different from another in the areas of:

- the quality of communication
- the power of presentation (benefits)
- the ideas applied to the product (applications).

The market today is being influenced by the growth of competition, takeovers and financial considerations. The quality of a salesperson's performance can therefore be seen to be vitally important. We must be better organised, knowledgeable, profit-orientated and skilled in the art of negotiation.

We live in an age of negotiation:

- Nations negotiate.
- Governments negotiate.
- Employers and unions negotiate.
- Husbands and wives negotiate.
- Parents and children negotiate.
- Sellers and buyers negotiate.

We all negotiate, sometimes several times a day. Look in any newspaper, somewhere someone is negotiating. Often the key to success in life is through good negotiation. The amazing thing is that as children we are expert negotiators, but for whatever reasons, we lose the skills as we grow older.

All types of negotiation have one thing in common which makes negotiating necessary:

> **The parties involved have varying degrees of power, but not absolute power over each other.**

Negotiation is about planning: very careful and detailed planning. Analyse any failed negotiation and you will find that inadequate planning was the likely cause.

Just offering a price concession is not negotiating.

Principles of negotiation

Definition of negotiation

Any good dictionary will give the definition of 'negotiation' as 'settle by dealing or bargaining; to arrange; to transfer; to confer with another, with a view to compromise'. Negotiation is an extension of selling.

What is negotiation

Probably the first point to appreciate about negotiating is that it is based on manoeuvring and movement by both parties. Within the negotiation process, priorities and objectives will change depending on what has been said and actions agreed. It is unlikely that people involved in negotiation will come out of it having achieved their ideal objectives. More than likely, it will be agreement achieved through compromise.

In every negotiation situation, you have something that the other person needs. Likewise, they will have something that you need, otherwise you would not be negotiating. But the very fact that you are, means that you have to live by a new set of rules.

From the beginning, a number of questions have to be answered:

- *Has the other person the authority you require?*
- *Is your aim and purpose clear and are you prepared to compromise as the negotiation progresses?*

And, probably the most important point:

- *Do you always try to achieve some pre-determined objective – even if it is not the one you set out to achieve?*

All too often, because we take the urgency of selling out of the negotiation situation, negotiations end without any true commitments.

Often the sentence 'Well, we did a lot of talking but we didn't really arrive at any decisions' can be heard. If this is the result of a negotiating session, particularly in the account situation, then it must be judged to be a failure. The account negotiators must be constantly aware of the objectives they are striving to achieve, although the interview may not end in complete acceptance of the proposal, be aware of what has been achieved on that particular occasion. For it may take many sessions to reach the final agreement.

Changing goals and strategy

Another factor of negotiating to be considered is that the deal may change many times during the negotiation. This means you have to listen very carefully to what your partner is saying. You cannot be too preoccupied with your own thoughts; you really have to listen to what your prospect is saying because you will base your next move on their words and thoughts.

In many ways negotiating can be likened to a game of chess. The individual who wins at chess is the person who watches and carefully responds to the other's moves. If it were played purely from an aggressive point of view, it is very unlikely that the game would be won.

So the account negotiator has to listen carefully to the statements and questions made and alter the deal accordingly as the negotiation progresses.

Establishing the aim

It is always wise to agree jointly the aim of each meeting. All too often negotiators lose their way because this aim was not established. If your buyer does not take the opportunity, then you must certainly introduce the aim of the negotiations at the beginning. This will help to do two things:

1 It will keep the conversation on beam during the first part of the negotiation.

2 It will enable you to bring the conversation back to the subject in hand, if as can often happen, it strays from the point.

The second factor is a key problem in the negotiating session. If the negotiation is to last for an hour, it is not uncommon to find that your partner will throw in 'red herrings' after the first ten minutes which could last for the next 40 minutes. Out of a true negotiating session of one hour you have achieved only 15 or 20 minutes of true negotiating about your subject.

To summarise, the three attitudes which must be adopted by each party in the negotiating situation are:

1 Acceptance that the deal may change as the negotiation progresses.

2 Acceptance that good negotiations are based on a true listening capability by each partner, but particularly the account negotiator.

3 The negotiation will have a true aim.

Knowledge and qualities required

Thomas Edison said 'Genius is one per cent inspiration and ninety-nine per cent perspiration.' Successful negotiating is 5% (or less) inspiration and 95% (or more) perspiration!

With few exceptions, the skills of successful negotiators can be developed. Weaknesses in any particular area, if they cannot be eradicated, may be minimised through the development of other strengths and capabilities.

Knowledge required by the successful negotiator

The account negotiator must, to be successful, acquire a great deal of knowledge. This is not only vital information in the negotiating situation, but also covers the necessary work and research outside the face to face negotiation.

Knowledge of the negotiator's company

- *What is the organisation structure?*
- *What is the directors and management structure?*
- *What is the ownership and financial structure?*
- *What are the parent, subsidiary and associated companies?*
- *What is the company policy – long and short term goals?*
- *What are department objectives?*
- *What is procedure and administration?*

Knowledge of the market

- *What is the market – total and by sector?*
- *What is expected to happen to the market – total and by sector?*
- *What is expected to happen to the company's share – total and by sector?*

Knowledge of the customers

- *Who are the company's customers (actual and potential)?*
- *Where are they located?*
- *How often do they buy?*
- *Which products/service are they currently buying and from whom?*
- *How do they finance?*
- *Who are the competitors' customers (actual and potential)?*
- *What are the buyer's needs?*
- *What is the likely point of agreement?*
- *What is the the value of your concessions?*
- *What are the benefits and value of your concessions to the buyer?*
- *What are the concessions the buyer is likely to offer?*
- *How can the cost of those concessions be minimised to the buyer?*
- *What is the buyer's likely initial stance?*

Knowledge of the competition

- *Who is the competition?*
- *What is their market share?*
- *What is expected to happen to their market share?*

Knowledge of the product

When negotiating, product knowledge is an essential feature of the negotiator's tool kit. They must know every single feature and benefit about their product and the negotiating situation calls for a great degree of skill in talking constructively about:

- what the product is
- its features
- the relevant benefits to the customer
- how it is made up
- its technical specification.

Questions such as these are vital to ensure that the negotiator is in possession of all the facts. The market trends, likely competitors' actions, targets and volumes, etc, are all essential tools of the trade as far as the negotiator is concerned. By asking ourselves these questions, we ensure that we are in a confident position during the negotiation situation.

Qualities of the successful negotiator

There are many qualities that a negotiator should possess, but probably the two most important are *empathy* and *projection*.

Empathy

Empathy has been described as 'seeing into somebody else's mind' or 'understanding the buyer's problems.'

But perhaps the best way of summing up 'empathy' is to say that the negotiator who possesses a great deal of empathy will create an atmosphere where the buyer almost sees his/her own views reflected through the negotiation. If negotiators can develop this skill in their operation, they will be able to convince with a great deal of success.

Projection

Projection can be described as:

- intensity of communication
- putting over an idea strongly or simply
- ensuring that the message is impressed strongly on the buyer's mind.

Naturally, projection will be tempered in the negotiation so that it does not monopolise, but successful negotiators have to appreciate that at times this is a quality that they will require.

Attitude

Almost as important to the negotiator, as in all commercial activity, are those qualities associated with a positive attitude:

- Enthusiasm.
- Initiative.
- Drive and determination.
- Self-discipline.
- Business sense.
- Optimism.
- Loyalty.
- Common sense (often in short supply).

Establishing objectives

In negotiating, as in any other subject, clear objectives are essential – but here the similarity between negotiating and any other type of objectives ends for in the account negotiating situation, the setting of objectives is completely different.

When setting objectives, the most important thing to appreciate is that in negotiating, unlike selling, there is no winner and no loser. In the selling situation, it is simply a matter of the salesperson selling the buyer a product or service. The salesperson may have to change the proposition slightly but, fundamentally, the objective remains a simple 'yes' to the salesperson's proposition, with predetermined guidelines.

Negotiating starts from the premise that two people will be 'discussing' a topic together. Objectives may change as the discussion progresses, dependent upon what is said by either partner; the account negotiator must not have only one objective but variable objectives that will ensure the success of their negotiation and the achievement of the ultimate aim.

The very first part of setting objectives is to define in clear terms, the ultimate objective that the negotiator is trying to achieve. Without these clear-cut objectives the discussion will soon get disjointed with 'red herrings' thrown in by the buyer to take emphasis away from the main points under discussion.

Therefore the account negotiator has to itemise objectives in three distinct areas:

1 Desirable objectives.

2 Probable objectives.

3 Essential objectives.

Defining the three types of objectives

Desirable objectives

Setting 'desirable objectives' will be what you the negotiator would ideally like to achieve as a result of the negotiation. They will be, by their very nature, optimistic, but nonetheless they will be targets and objectives that are desirable and possible to achieve.

When setting objectives at this stage, you must avoid setting too difficult or impossible objectives which are idealistic and unrealistic, but in this category a negotiator must be optimistic.

Probable objectives

Under this category are those objectives that are not as optimistic as the desirable ones. However, they do represent what will be a satisfactory solution and would certainly give you the profitable solution you wish for yourself and your company.

Essential objectives

Finally, we have those objectives that are essential to the outcome of the discussion. They are the very basic requirements of the whole discussion and without these being achieved any success from the negotiation is in question.

In the following example we have the introduction of a new product to an account which represents a substantial share of the company's business:

Introduction of a new product to a major multiple account

Desirable objectives:

- 100 per cent distribution in all outlets at a competitive retail selling price.
- Agreement for ideal location.
- Obtain displays in five of the largest outlets.

Probable objectives:

- Secure an initial order at a realistic price.
- Obtain permission for local sales personnel to discuss space and display opportunities at individual outlets.

Essential objectives:

- Obtain an initial order for a trial period in five branches. ·

Here you have the fundamentals of the triple objectives in action. Throughout the negotiation, the negotiator will be bearing in mind that the minimum objective to achieve is a trial period in five branches. However, having started from the premise of achieving the desirable objectives, the whole negotiation will slowly come together until the negotiator finally ends up with the essential objective.

If a negotiator has achieved either the probable objectives or the desirable objectives, or even a mixture of the two, the result of the negotiation will be within the planned band.

Time objectives

It may be that acceptance of a particular product or service is going to take three or four sessions of negotiating. When this happens, the negotiator's essential objectives are to achieve certain steps at each negotiating session.

The outcomes of negotiation

Whenever and with whoever you are negotiating, there are three potential outcomes. The implications of each needs to be carefully considered. The ultimate aim of any negotiation must be that each partner's fundamental needs have been met – a 'win/win' situation. All too often, after a negotiation is completed, one party will feel that they have got the worst end of the deal and feel clearly aggrieved – a 'win/lose' situation. This is often the result of short-term thinking with little consideration for long-term commercial relationships.

Total intransigence, unrealistic aims and a complete disregard for the future, are the hallmarks of failure, resulting in a 'lose/lose' situation.

Although not every negotiation will end in success, the process of terminating a negotiation needs to be carefully managed to avoid any recriminations and apportioning of blame which could prove inhibiting to future opportunities.

If, however, such a situation should occur, evaluate the likely causes. Potential causes are:

- poor planning
- lack of knowledge of customers and their needs
- unrealistic aims and objectives
- inflexibility
- poor negotiating skills
- lack of authority
- negotiating with the wrong person
- entering into the negotiation in the first place – was there a basis for negotiation?

The three outcomes of negotiations

1 **Characteristics of win/win situation:**

- Achieved by joint decision.
- Meets needs of both parties.
- Decision is not unacceptable to either party.
- Requires two-way communication.
- Emphasis is on flexible approaches.
- Concentrates on the key aims.

2 **Characteristics of win/lose situation:**

- The creation of an 'us and them' distinction between the parties.
- Individuals' attitude directed only towards victory.
- Own point of view only.
- Strong emphasis on immediate solutions regardless of whether the long-term aims are met.
- Potential damage to long-term commercial credibility.

3 **Characteristics of lose/lose situation:**

- Aims of either party not achieved.
- Disillusionment with the negotiating process.
- Frustration.
- Long-term relationship damaged.
- No solutions generated.
- Inadequate planning/research.

Opening the negotiation

Establishing initial aims

Establishing from the start the joint aims and objectives and time frames, is fundamental to the negotiation process. Have both parties the authority to conclude the deal, or is there a point where other people from either side will need to become involved?

Common agreement – initial stance

It makes sound sense at the commencement of any negotiation to identify those areas where there is clear common agreement. This in itself creates a positive and collaborative environment. It is then important to identify those areas where there are gaps identified from the initial stance, that is, to gain agreement on those areas where there is apparent disagreement. Often this will be a sound objective for the first meeting. In this way both parties will have time to reflect on and consider future areas where they may be prepared to compromise. Rushing the negotiation at this stage could be fatal.

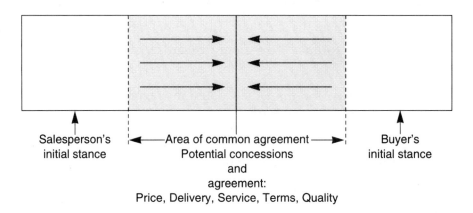

Salesperson's initial stance ← Area of common agreement → Buyer's initial stance

Potential concessions and agreement:
Price, Delivery, Service, Terms, Quality

Probing questions

The skill of asking questions is particularly useful in a negotiation situation. Once the initial stance has been established, the skilled negotiator must open two-way conversation. You need to understand why the buyer has made particular statements and to probe for likely areas of compromise. Asking carefully constructed and searching questions will often yield a wealth of information and will often result in buyers modifying their demands. It will also signal to the buyer that you are interested in clarifying the situation and looking for potential areas of compromise.

Of the two types of questioning techniques, *open questions* should effectively stimulate discussion and meaningful answers. *Closed questions*, which may result in a simple yes or no response, can stifle conversation and lead to intransigent and negative attitudes – the very opposite of what is required in the negotiation. At this stage, keep an open mind and infer that everything is negotiable. Remember the whole package and avoid getting bogged down and side-tracked into an area of serious disagreement.

The key is to agree.

- Agree on the issues where no problems exist.
- Agree on the issues that need to be discussed.

Remember, you are negotiating, not scoring points. Through the use of open questions, search for the variables. Search for those areas that are important to the customer. Remember that contrary to the view taken by many so-called negotiators, it is not always just a question of price.

Potential areas of customer needs:

- Savings in costs.
- Increased output.
- Reliable service.
- Commissioning package.
- More efficiency.
- Improved cash flow.
- Improved profit.

- Greater liability.
- Increased range.
- Innovation.
- Marketing support.
- Increased output.
- Improved labour/customer relations.

Remember the price reflects the total package and support, not just the product. Present to the buyers what they need, not what you think they need.

Signalling

During the questioning stage you need to listen. All too often, the negotiator may lack the ability to do this. You need to listen to buyers' responses, which could signal that they may be prepared to move, for example: 'I could not possibly agree to take that quantity in one delivery', or 'We normally expect three months' credit.' These are clear indications that although these are references to past experience, in the present situation, the buyer may be prepared to compromise.

At this stage, you may wish to convey with similar signals that you also have potential areas of movement. The point has now been reached where both parties have signalled that they may move, although they have not declared to what extent.

Examples of the hidden language of signals

'We would find it extremely difficult to stop selling 'x' product.'	– Not impossible.
'These are our standard terms.'	– They are negotiable.
'It is not our normal practice to take on new suppliers until the end of the year.'	– So who's normal?
'We can discuss that point.'	– It's negotiable.
'We could not accept that quantity in that time period.'	– I'm prepared to negotiate on price, delivery, quantity.

Bargaining and making concessions

Once the signals have been given and received, you can now move into the bargaining phase. This is often referred to as the 'big if'. For example:

> *'If you agree to x then I will agree to y.'*
> *'If you agree to increase your order to x over three deliveries, I will reduce the price by five per cent.'*

Through a process of 'if' statements, both parties are moving through compromise, to a point where agreement can be reached – **a win/win situation**.

Both parties are feeling that they have gained benefits.

This is the skill of making concessions. Whenever the negotiator introduces a concession into the discussion, it must be used with a clearly signalled condition that any concession will require something in return from the buyer. If too many concessions are given without reciprocation, the buyer will simply keep asking for more and refuse to move on until the concession is given. It is generally accepted that it is better if the concession comes first and the condition second. In this way the buyer finds it difficult to isolate the concession and ignore the condition.

The value of the concession

Consider the value of your concession in the buyer situation. What may be of little value to you could be significant to the buyer. Equally buyers can be easily irritated if your so-called high value concession is not equally valued by them.

Closing the deal

When all points are resolved, summarise the agreed points and close the deal. It is good practice in all negotiations to confirm in writing the precise details of the negotiation to reduce any areas of misunderstanding and the likelihood of hearing the phrase 'There was just one small point.'

Team negotiation

While all the principles and processes remain the same, additional rules come into play when the sales negotiation is accompanied by supporting colleagues.

The key rules are:

- The customer is advised in advance as to who is attending the meeting and why.
- All should be clear about their roles in the meeting and be prepared to speak when asked.
- Decide who is to take the lead role and indicate when someone is to speak.
- Decide on the procedure and who will be responsible for taking notes.
- Only one person should speak at a time.
- In front of a customer the team should never convey internal disagreement.

- When in doubt have an adjournment or minute the point for a further meeting.
- The message from your team needs to be consistent.
- Create a way of communicating to one another non-verbally, for example, signals, notes, etc.

Remember team negotiating can be a powerful process if well prepared. However, if it is ill-disciplined and disorganised, it can seriously damage you and your company's credibility.

THE NEGOTIATOR'S CHECKLIST

Techniques for making proposals:

- Goodwill concessions toughen the other person's responses.

- ONO (Or Nearest Offer) weakens your bargaining position.

- Don't give discounts to people who need your business.

- The negotiator's most useful two-letter word is 'if'. Preface all your propositions with 'if':

  'If you agree to this, then I will agree to that'.

- There is no such thing as a fixed price tag:

  'How much off for cash?'
  'How much off if I combine the purchases?'

  (and don't accept their first offer!) Don't change the price, change the packaging.

- Packaging is the best defence to a price challenge.

Responding to proposals:

- Never accept a negotiator's first offer.

- Don't just state an objection, negotiate a remedy.

- Never concede anything without getting something back in exchange.

- Remember, absolutely nothing is given away free.

- Can you afford to 'split the difference'?

- If they want something from you, gain a concession.

- Put a price on demands.

- If you haven't got a principle – invent one.

Behaviour for negotiators:

- Tempers are never calmed by being tested.

Continued overleaf

> - Tough negotiators open high, stick close to their openings and make few, small, concessions. They are not afraid of deadlock.
>
> - Soft negotiators open modestly, move a long way, and frequently make large concessions. They are terrified of deadlock.
>
> - Amateurs are given to using clumsy threats.

Negotiating: the golden rules

- Aim high. You can always trade down, never up.
- Get the other person's *total* shopping list *before* you start negotiating by using open questions.
- Keep the *whole* package in mind the *whole* time.
- Keep searching for variables (to vary any dogmatic approach).
- Don't let your concentration wander.

Ten negotiating principles

- Never *give* a concession. Trade it reluctantly – for one of equal, or greater, value.
- Leave the other person feeling they have done a good deal, too.
- Watch for danger phrases: 'One small point....' 'Fairer to both sides....' 'It's in your interest'.
- Once you start backing down, it's a job to climb up again.
- Maintain *neutrality* in the early stages. You are there to reach agreement.
- Absorb an 'attack' by making notes.
- If you want to think, read over your notes or telephone the office.
- Never make an offer until you have the cost-list of everything they intend to argue about. *'Is there anything else that represents a departure from the quotation?'*
- All deadlines are negotiable.
- Anything the other person accepts and puts forward as a 'constant' can nearly always be made into a variable.

General principles of negotiating

- Make a negotiator happy – negotiate.
- Good negotiators face the same problems as everybody else.
- In negotiation generosity is not contagious.
- Negotiating is about trading not conceding.
- In negotiating both sides have a veto.
- Negotiating involves both partners in a commitment to a joint decision.
- Because it's 'fair', it doesn't make it 'equal'.
- If you believe they have the power, they have. But then so do you.

Don'ts in negotiating

Don't:

- make assumptions
- accept anybody's first offer
- state grievances
- treat it as win/lose
- get personal
- make 'goodwill' concessions
- pitch too low

- score points
- use ONO
- walk out
- make the other party feel a loser
- negotiate if you don't have to
- be intimidated
- over-commit.

The eight stages of effective negotiation

1 Research

- Background of the company, brands, products, marketing strategy.
- Trading area.
- Current supplier.
- Key personnel, etc.

2 Preparation

- Buyer's likely needs.
- Your needs – desirable, probable, essential.

- Value of your concessions.
- Benefits of your concessions that increase the value.
- The concession they are likely to give and how the cost to them can be minimised.
- The buyer's likely initial stance.
- Likely objections and how they can be overcome.
- How you will move them from their opening stance to the point of agreement.
- The likely areas of eventual agreement.

3 Opening

- Create a receptive climate.
- Agree agenda for discussion.

4 Question

- Establish needs and initial stance.
- Probe for areas they may concede.
- What is important to the customer.
- What are the customer's key requirements? For example:
  - savings in costs
  - increased output
  - improved cash flow
  - more efficiency
  - improvement in profit return
  - greater reliability
  - increased range
  - innovations.

5 Signalling

- Expose areas of movement.
- Signals from either party.
- Listen for the signals.

6 Bargaining

- Moves towards compromise.
- Use 'if' and 'suppose'.
- Remove areas of resistance.

7 Conclude

- Summarise.
- Agree all actions and time frames.

8 Follow-up

- Confirm all agreements and actions.

Activity 9

Negotiation evaluation

Evaluate three recent negotiation situations, against the three potential outcomes and explain your reasoning. Were they

1 Win/win?

2 Win/lose?

3 Lose/lose?

If 2 or 3, with the benefit of hindsight, in what way would you have handled the situation differently?

Activity 10

Negotiation planning

List six existing or potential customers with whom you will be entering into negotiations in the future.

Prepare for each negotiation your

- preferred, probable and essential outcomes
- likely areas of concessions.

Visual sales aids

A picture is worth a thousand words. The power of television advertising is an indisputable fact. Visual communication is the most powerful way to hold people's attention and to influence behaviour. This principle applies equally to selling. However competent you are at selling or superior your company, product or service, you will not sell really effectively unless you gain and maintain the full interest and attention of your customer.

There are few people who have the ability to paint word pictures. Visual selling aids are vital tools to support and increase the impact and benefits of your ideas. With skilful use they can also appeal to the human senses of sight, touch, even smell and taste: powerful communication factors.

The benefits of visual sales aids can be summarised as follows:

- To clarify a point which may be difficult to explain.
- To support, prove and reinforce your presentation.
- To help the customer remember the key points.

Only use as many visual selling aids as are needed to fulfil these three aims.

Visual sales aids include:

- the product
- samples
- demonstrations
- advertisements
- TV or radio advertising schedules
- customer record cards
- price lists
- catalogues, brochures etc.
- drawings, plans
- sales presenter
- photographs
- audio, video tapes
- technical data
- press releases
- site visits to see product or service in operation
- third party testimony
- a note pad
- pen or pencil.

Many salespeople create their own visual aids to suit their own industry and even individual customers. Providing they look professional, they can be the most effective.

Knowledge required when using visual aids:

- Be aware of what visual aids are available.
- Have a full understanding of their content and what they say.
- Be fully competent when conducting demonstrations.

Failing on these points can cause loss of credibility and confidence in the customer's mind.

Skills and points to watch when using visual sales aids

- Keep your visual aids out of sight until they are needed. Once used, put them away. Visual aids left in reach of the customer after they have been used, can distract and possibly cause the customer to miss an important point in your presentation.
- Keep control of the visual aid wherever possible. The further you are away from the visual aid, the less you can control its use and the interview.
- Should the buyer wish to take time to look at the visual aid, stop talking until he or she has done so. Retrieve control of the visual aid and continue. Wherever possible, when using brochures, leaflets, etc., keep one hand on the open page, using the free hand to point with a pen.
- Always use a pen or pencil to point to specific items. Never use your finger.
- Only use one visual aid at a time.
- Keep them clean and in pristine condition.
- Use visual aids selectively. Do not use more than are necessary. Too many confuse the customer.

Activity 11

Developing your visual sales aids

- Carry out a complete review of all your visual sales aids.
- How do they support your presentation?

Making effective group sales presentations

In the majority of cases, sales personnel are trained to deal with sales situations involving selling to one buyer. In these sales/negotiating meetings there is often a degree of informality and feedback from the buyer in the form of questions and answers to questions. Now the salesperson must be highly competent and professional in group selling and negotiation and making effective presentations. If you are not equipped and prepared for such challenges then you will consciously or unconsciously avoid these situations even when opportunities arise.

There are two main hurdles or fears you will have to overcome in preparing yourself to handle such multiple-sales challenges. First, the risk of being exposed to cross-questioning if you actively seek feedback from qualified technical people; and second, the lack of any evidence of success when making presentations.

These two factors must be controlled or eliminated if you want to capitalise on the opportunities. Group selling meetings and presentations offer you the opportunity to sell effectively and successfully to a large number of people at one time. The first step in developing this skill is to consider a number of key questions.

Who is likely to become involved in the buying and selling process and decision? In both buying and selling situations many people are involved in decisions:

Buying companies	Selling companies
Directors	Sales directors
Purchasing officers/buyers	Sales personnel
Marketing staff	Sales managers
Technical staff	Marketing/product managers
Quality Assurance staff	Technical advisers
Operations/distribution staff	Installers/contractors
Computer staff	Financial analysts
Accountants	Computer staff
	Operations/distribution staff

Who should take part in group meetings and presentations? Considerable thought and care must be taken to choose the 'best' team to attend such group meetings or to make group presentations so that subsequent buyer relationships run smoothly. The following factors should be borne in mind:

- *What type of meeting is it?*
- *What will be the status and decision-making powers of those present from the buying group?*
- *What are the expectations of the buying group that will be attending?*
- *What type of decisions will the meeting reach?*
- *What technical expertise will the meeting possess in the buying group?*
- *What technical expertise, therefore, will it require from your side?*
- *Can one person handle the meeting or should a group attend?*
- *If a buying decision is likely to be made at the meeting, who will manage the resulting contract?*
- *If a group is to present to the buying group, who should lead the group?*

Remember that the on-going relationships with the customer will require the build-up and establishment of credibility of whoever will be chosen for this role and that the internal motivation of the salesperson/sales team must be considered.

Planning the group presentation

The planning of such group meetings and presentations is in two stages. First, the planning and preparation stage. Second, the conduct and implementation stage. There are two sets of factors to be considered at the planning and preparation stage: the business aims and objectives and critical human factors. The latter are the more difficult but if they are not considered can not only ruin one meeting but reduce the chances of a second one ever taking place and consequently damage long-term relationships.

Objective factors

- *What results do you want the meeting to achieve? (Ideal results? Minimum results?)*

- *What will you present and discuss to reach this objective?*
- *How will you present them?*
- *In what order will you present them?*
- *What key questions need to be asked and who will ask them?*
- *In what order/at what stage should they be asked?*
- *What visual/display material should be prepared?*
- *How will it be used?*
- *Who is to be involved? Are they clear about their role and responsibility?*
- *Who is to take the lead?*

Subjective factors

- *Who will take part in the meeting?*
- *Who should be persuaded/influenced to take part?*
- *What do they think they know?*
- *What do they really know?*
- *What do they expect?*
- *Who is likely to be an ally?*
- *Who is likely to be an opponent?*
- *Who is likely to be neutral or indifferent?*
- *How can these people be influenced or guided?*
- *What further research needs to be conducted to fully answer the above subjective factors?*

Human factors to be considered when presenting to groups

Salespeople can be:	*Buyers can be:*
Information givers or just talkers	Hostile, recalcitrant
Information getters, listeners	Self important, 'Mr Big'
Negative, nervous, afraid	Jokers, nervous, apologetic
Meek, apologetic	Silent
Brash, 'Mr Big', too positive, overpowering	Sceptical, suspicious
Mature, poised, friendly, confident	Slow, methodical
	Mature, poised, thoughtful
	Decisive
	Impulsive

Jokers, over-friendly   Mr Average
Impulsive   Over-cautious
Neutral, friendly   Needing constant reassurance
Goodwill order-taker

These factors highlight the importance of analysing the attitudes, knowledge, status, position, personalities, of all those whom the selling team will meet at the presentation.

Bear in mind that even people you may know well on an individual basis are likely to adjust the way they behave as individuals to the role they play or are expected to play at the presentation meeting. Beware in particular of the subordinate in a buying group who promises to pursue a certain policy or course of action at a meeting at which his/her manager or managing director suddenly decides to be present. The power to hire and fire can sometimes result in promises being forgotten and your erstwhile ally turning into an opponent.

What support will be required?

Most group meetings require support material and visual sales aids and the form these should take must be planned. For example:

- Agenda
- Folders, with background about people, products, etc.
- Samples
- Briefing of staff involved in providing support
- Equipment, for example, flip charts, overhead projector, 35 mm projector, screen.

Implementing the group presentation

Whatever type of group presentation is to be made or meeting conducted, it requires structure throughout to reflect three factors:

1 Recognition by you that your audience as a whole and each individual member of it wants to feel important and be respected and for you to recognise this in your behaviour and conduct.

2 Ability through your words, your actions, your handling of questions and the solutions you propose to show understanding of the customer situation needs.

3 Creation of trust and confidence in you, in your company and in your solutions.

These factors pose challenging problems when presenting a proposition more formally to a group or to a larger audience. Frequently at the conclusion of a successful round of negotiation meetings, the supplying company is asked to present the proposition agreed to the board of directors of the buying company or to the sales force. In such situations your presentation must be well planned, structured around the needs and expectations of your audience and offer solutions in *their* terms.

PLANNING A GROUP PRESENTATION
LOCATION/VENUE CHECKLIST

Room

- Size
- Layout
- Chairs
- Tables
- Lighting
- Electrical sockets
- Window blinds

Audience requirements

- Notepaper/pencils
- Product information
- Refreshments
- Samples

Audience

- Notified – briefed

Meeting agenda

- Finalise by
- Circulated

Meeting budget

- £ amount
- Approved

MEETING PLANNING PROGRAMME CHECKLIST

- Meeting aims
- Information to be presented
- Methods
- Visual aids
- Key discussion points

- Handouts – samples
- Possible objections
- Commitments planned
- Timing

Consider the listener's point of view

One of the results of the growth in communications, particularly those involving the visual senses, is that people have become accustomed to certain standards of performance from those who address them. They may not agree with what is being said, they may not even be interested, but they will not fail to judge the style and competence displayed by the presenters. The audience remember the image long after they have forgotten the content.

Consequently it is unacceptable and commercially naive to say that any form of presentation will do. Rightly or wrongly an audience, whatever its composition, will judge presenters' abilities and those of the company by the way presenters conduct themselves. This is not to say that the substance of a speaker's proposals is unimportant, rather that the impact is disproportionately enhanced or diminished by the quality of the presentation. You are in a sense only as good as the ideas for which you gain acceptance. There are four categories of speakers:

1 Those who do not bother about what they are going to say or how they are going to say it.

2 Those who 'put on a show', but convey very little.

3 Those whose material is good, but poorly presented.

4 Those who have something worthwhile to say and present it well.

The judge of a presentation is the audience. No two audiences are the same. The individuals within an audience differ in their attitude but, whatever their personalties and job responsibilities may be, they all react to presentations. There are certain mental demands which have to be met before they give their acceptance. In addition, they are influenced by what they see, hear and feel. All these can be summarised as the listener's viewpoint and expectations. These elements form a sequence from which a speaker can prepare a structure for the presentation.

The thinking sequence that the listener's mind follows consists of seven points. A presentation must be mindful of them all.

1 *I am important and want to be respected*

Each member of the audience wants the respect of the speaker. Without it the speaker is lost.

2 *Consider my needs*

Any proposal is evaluated by the listeners in terms of their own priorities and values. These are determined by what they want to achieve:

- in their work
- as a person.

The content of a presentation will have little impact if the listeners cannot see commercial and personal benefits. In a business context their needs will be related to improved profitability, increased sales, reduced costs, etc. They will want to know early in a presentation that they can relate to the theme. If so, they will give the presenter their attention and interest. Consequently the final decision will rest on the answer to one question: 'Will my needs be met by these people and their proposals?'

3 *Will your ideas help me?*

If their attention and interest have been gained, will they be keen to know how the presenter's proposals will help them to achieve the end results they are looking for? What will the presenter's proposals do for them and their company?

4 *What are the facts?*

This step in the thinking process arises from the previous one. They want to know how the presenter proposes to ensure that the promised results are realistic. Depending on the situation they may also want evidence that the projected results have been achieved in other similar situations.

5 *What are the snags?*

It is an integral part of the listeners' decision-making process that they will consider possible disadvantages arising from the presenter's proposals. Any that come to mind which they cannot see being resolved they will inevitably voice in the form of objections. In a group situation, however, there is a likelihood that objections to the presenter's proposals will not be openly voiced.

6 What shall I do?

Provided all previous points have been covered they are now faced with a decision: 'Do I accept or reject these proposals?' In making the choice each listener concentrates on individual needs, job or personal situation and decides accordingly. If they have several sets of proposals to consider, they will prefer the ones which in their eyes best meet their needs.

7 I approve

If these points have been satisfactorily handled from the listeners' point of view, they will make a decision in the presenter's favour.

The importance of the listener's point of view

The seven points mentioned above represent the path that the human mind takes before giving willing approval to proposals. The problem facing presenters, however, is that by nature they have difficulty in presenting their proposals in that kind of sequence and with that kind of emphasis. In many situations where proposals are being presented speakers concentrate on their company and their ideas while the audience is more interested in what they want to achieve. Consequently the audience often loses interest, their attention wanes, and they reject both the proposals and the presenter.

By structuring the presentation around the listeners' attention and interest, persuading them of the value to them of their proposals and resolving their objections and concerns they can be drawn to accept the presenter's proposals.

Other considerations

When presented with proposals, the human mind not only thinks along certain lines, it is influenced by what it sees and hears. To a lesser extent it is affected by sensations of touch, taste and smell. In formal presentations *sight* and *hearing* are the most influential senses.

Sight

Listeners react to their first visual impact of you as a presenter. They expect your dress, expressions and gestures to match the environment and the content of your presentation. They look for signs of confidence. Consider the position from the listeners' viewpoint. They see:

- How you are dressed. Are you dressed appropriately? Will your clothes distract your audience from what you have to say to them?
- Your mannerisms. Always be yourself, but avoid distracting mannerisms. Some presenters wave their arms up and down while talking. Gestures should be controlled and only used to emphasise specific points.

Listeners find it much easier to concentrate on and take greater interest in the things they can see. However, what they look at must be understandable, simple and professionally handled. They have greater confidence in a presenter who looks at them. *Make eye contact.* Keep in touch with your audience by looking at them.

Hearing

There are two major differences between a public presentation and a normal conversation. During a conversation you can ask your listeners if they understand what you have just said, or alternatively they can ask you to repeat something if they need clarification. However, in a public presentation this is not always possible or there may not be any interruptions by the audience. So you have to make sure that you get your message across and understood *the first time*. For these reasons, remember the following points:

- Speak louder than you would in normal conversation. Adapt the scale of your presentation to the size of the room and to the size of your audience so that *everyone* hears you.
- Always make sure you pronounce words distinctly and emphasise the last words in each sentence. Inexperienced presenters have a habit of fading at the end of each sentence. If it contains a key part of your message and no one hears you, your presentation has failed.

- Audiences expect you to speak in language they can understand. Avoid jargon which might confuse people.
- Don't speak too fast.
- Vary the pace and pitch of your voice to maintain people's attention and interest.
- Use **pauses**. Nothing is more effective in a presentation than the pause. It gives the audience time to digest what you have just said or shown, and gives you time to pick up the substance of your next point. It holds an audience expectant at what you will say next.
- People dislike having to concentrate on a presentation that is being read.

Presentation planning

Why prepare?

Presentations are selling situations. They are also unnatural social relationships because:

- the presenters have usually sought out their listeners
- the presenters want them to act in their favour
- the presenters may have to change the listeners' ideas
- the presenters will often feel out on their own.

These situations can create tension, which makes the presenter act out of character by talking too quickly, avoiding eye contact with the audience, concentrating on his/her ideas rather than on the audience's needs. Planning helps to reduce tension and ensures an audience-related presentation based on their requirements rather than your own.

What should you prepare?

Since planning is simply the thinking process that precedes positive action, the first thing is to define your aim. This can be a long-term aim covering a series of presentations or a single aim for one session. Having got your aim, you can consider the structure of the presentation. For simplicity this structure should be based on the listener's point of view and divided into three main parts: the *beginning*, the *middle* and the *end*.

Listener's point of view	Structure	Preparation points
I am important and want to be respected. Consider my needs.	**Beginning**	Gaining attention. Building rapport. Statement of theme/aim.
Will your ideas help me?	**Middle**	Points to be made. How they will benefit the audience.
What are the facts?		Support material: examples; third party references; visual aids.
What are the snags?		Possible audience objections: answers.
What shall I do?	**End**	Resume of theme/aim. Audience needs. Summary of points.
I approve.		Closing words: commitment.

How does a structure help?

Apart from reducing tension and ensuring an audience-orientated presentation, a structure has other important advantages for a presenter:

- It enables the audience to follow easily, because it is based on an initial outline of the aim/theme, followed by development of that theme and concluded by a summary of the theme, and the points made, with a request for action.
- It ensures every mental demand by the audience is covered.
- It provides a framework to fall back on if the audience leads the presenter astray.
- It provides a disciplined and logical basis on which the presenter can plan the presentation.

The needs of your audience

Sit down with a pen and pad and imagine you are already in front of your audience, Ask yourself several questions:

- *Who are they?*
- *What are their needs as business people and as individuals?*
- *How much do they already know about the subject?*
- *What do they need to know that I can tell them?*
- *What are their backgrounds, culture, level of intelligence?*

Preparing your notes

One of the most important skills to develop is setting down what you want to say in notes to which you can refer easily. The constraint of following a detailed script, means that your eyes are focused on this and you are not holding the attention of your audience. For a complex talk write out what you plan to say in detail then select the key sentences or words that summarise each section and put these either on to cards or into checklist form on paper.

Conducting the presentation: the beginning

At the start of your presentation you have to achieve three *objectives*:

1 Gain the undivided attention of your audience.

2 Build rapport between you and your audience.

3 State the aim/theme in terms of the needs of your audience.

Objective 1: To gain the undivided attention of your audience

Before you start speaking the first impact you make on your audience will be through your appearance and manner. Audiences tend to make quick judgements on first appearances. It is important to:

- **Stand up straight** in a comfortable stance with your feet slightly apart.
- **Look at your audience** in a confident manner. It helps if you have learned your opening sentences by heart so that you do not at the

very outset, when you want to hold your audience's attention, bury your head in your notes.

- **Talk louder than is necessary for normal conversation.** You have to make instant impact when you speak, so your voice must be projected.

When appropriate drama, curiosity, a story, a checklist, or questions can be used to attract audience attention, for example:

Dramatic openings

Dame Agnes Weston, who will always be remembered by seamen for her work in collecting money for the Missions to Seamen, often found herself making appeals for money in church halls. If, when she was about to speak, she felt the audience needed galvanising, she would deliberately knock over the lectern which was conveniently placed near her foot. The crash as it hit the floor brought all the audience to the edge of their chairs and also woke those who were asleep!

Another excellent use of drama was used by a presenter to show the value of training: 'Yesterday a plane, in which my wife was one of the 120 passengers, crash-landed at Heathrow Airport. My wife and her travelling companions owe their lives to the thousands of pounds spent on training the pilot of that aircraft who knew in that moment of crisis, when the undercarriage failed to operate, how to bring the aircraft in to land with the greatest chance of saving the lives of those on board. In that moment his training "paid a massive dividend".'

Curious openings

A pension insurance broker, presenting his scheme to a board of directors, took off the wrist-watch he was wearing and with great ceremony placed it in a glass full of water saying: 'On the back it says "this watch is waterproof". Let us see if the maker's guarantee stands up to the test of its promise. It is about the guarantees behind the pension scheme you are considering today, that I want to talk.'

A story opening

A short interesting story, well told and containing the message you want to convey, or which is linked to the theme of your presentation, can focus attention. Asked to explain 'why marketing is necessary' a sales director began: 'My company once sent me to America and I travelled to New York on the liner Queen Mary. It was at the height of the season, yet the ship was barely half full of passengers. As I puzzled over this on a walk round the deck on the first day out from Southampton, I glanced up into the sky and saw two aircraft winging their way in the same direction as this great ship. And then the penny dropped: overhead flew Queen Mary's erstwhile passengers and presumably her profits. That convinced me that marketing is necessary – that we need to look at tomorrow and ask ourselves how will we stay in business?'

A checklist

Another effective opening is to use a checklist which then becomes the framework of your subsequent presentation, for example: 'Ladies and Gentlemen, you state that first you need to increase profitability – this scheme will help you do so. Second, you need the security of on-going business – this will give you it. Third, you want to be linked with a successful product – you can be.'

Objective 2: To build rapport between you and your audience

A part of the secret of any successful presentation lies in the relationship between you and your audience. Your audience must warm to you. Never let it be said of you: 'He had everything except one thing. Nobody believed he believed'. Depending on the circumstances, one or more of the following will help build rapport.

Compliments. If your audience belong to a company that has achieved something notable you can express your admiration or compliment on it. However, compliments paid must be genuine and specific. Anyone can offer empty praises.

Mention a common interest. If you and your audience have things in common these can be mentioned. They can be either social or business. For example: 'As an engineer it is a great pleasure today for me to be amongst professional colleagues.' Demonstrate your competence, without boasting.

Radiate enthusiasm – it will make your audience enthusiastic. In your tone of voice, the occasional smile, you can bring a warmth to your presentation which is catching.

Objective 3: To state the theme/aim in terms of the needs of your audience

This is very important because it sets the tone of the whole presentation. For maximum impact the theme should be stated, where possible, in terms of audience needs, for example, addressing a company's top management:

> 'With competition in your industry becoming stronger and the pressure on profit margins increasing every day, the effectiveness of the people in your sales marketing team is crucial to your success. It is about their performance and how it can be improved that I wish to talk to you today'.

Not: 'I'd like to talk about our ideas on marketing and sales training'.

In short, if they don't understand what the subject means to them they will lose interest.

If the presentation is going to cover several points it is helpful to mention them at the beginning so that the audience knows what they can expect.

The opening of a presentation sets the scene for everything that follows. You, the presenter, want the audience to have confidence in you and want their undivided attention. Above all you want them to believe that you have something that they will want to know. To achieve these things you have to appear confident, enthusiastic and keen to help them. Above all else, remember this golden rule when preparing your opening words:

You only get one chance to make a good first impression.

Conducting the presentation: the middle

The four objectives to achieve in the middle of your presentation:

1 To present the proposals in detail.

2 To have each point accepted.

3 To maintain attention.

4 To prevent or handle objections.

Objective 1: To present the proposals in detail

By this time the audience will know the theme of your presentation, and, if it has been stated in terms of their needs, they expect to be informed of the ways in which you propose to meet them.

To ensure clarity and to aid acceptance it is best to take one point at a time and deal with it before moving on to the next. This can be done in two ways, depending on the subject matter. Either take each of the audience needs at a time and present the ideas you have for meeting that need, or take each of your ideas at a time and show how it meets their needs. When the subject matter permits, it is better to structure the presentation around audience needs because these are the things uppermost in their minds.

Objective 2: To have each point accepted

Acceptance of your points depends on their being understood, being seen to be of value in that they will produce a desirable result, being known to be valid, and being agreed.

Understanding can be achieved by:

- using language familiar to the audience, avoiding jargon
- explaining ideas by using similes, or going into detail
- using actions or gestures.

Always make sure that an action or gesture does help to communicate the point you are making. To extend both arms to indicate massive size will be effective if you have not used this gesture before. If you have been waving them about all the time then it will not. Leaning forward on the desk from which you are speaking and then stating a serious point can be most effective if your audience has so far not seen you do this.

Giving demonstrations

Nothing directs the attention of an audience from one point to another so surely as a physical demonstration, or showing a piece of equipment. However, always take your time, tell your audience what you are going to do before you start, and give your reasons for doing it.

Using visual aids

Like demonstrations, visual aids, skilfully introduced, can convey information, convince audiences and hold their attention. Keep in mind some basic rules about visual aids: uniformity of size is preferable; readability from the back of the room is essential. Always go to the farthest point in the room and check that what you are showing can be seen and understood by everyone. If your visuals are not uniform in size then you must carry out this check for each one you propose showing.

Avoid too much detail on one visual aid. Whether it is a chart or a slide, keep information to about four lines and make letters three inches high. Sketches, pictures or diagrams linked to words convey your visual message more effectively. Keep numerical information on charts to the minimum. People cannot remember it. Use as few words as possible so that each one makes impact.

Don't apologise for your visuals; just make sure they are good. Keep them hidden until needed. If you are showing a series of charts, then have the top one covered by at least two thicknesses of plain paper and interleave between the others you propose showing. This avoids the danger of the outline of your visual aids being seen through the flimsy chart paper that is sometimes supplied.

Perhaps you wish to illustrate a specific point and give impact to your presentation by drawing a diagram or writing key points or figures on the flip chart. If you are not confident that you will be able to recall the material from memory, take an HB pencil and very faintly draw onto the flip chart paper the drawing you wish to reproduce. If you want to write boldly in magic marker pen three or four key points, then faintly write in pencil the words in the top right-hand corner of the flip chart. From a distance your audience will not see or be aware of your prepared prompters. They provide you with the guides you need without having to rush back to your notes all the time. Number each visual you propose showing and place the relevant visual aid number beside the points in your notes where you want to show each one.

Allow your audience to see your visuals without distraction. Too many speakers ruin the impact of their excellent visuals by competing with them. A picture is worth a thousand words. Show each one and *shut up* while your audience takes in what you want to communicate.

Remove your visual aids when they have served their purpose. This rule is broken by so many speakers. Overhead projectors are left on, flip charts left with picturers on them, a model remains visible to the audience when the speaker has moved on in the presentation to deal with points totally unrelated to what these visual aids are saying. The result is that the attention of some members of the audience is distracted, and if the speaker is becoming boring, often the important things they want to say are missed. Afterwards they blame the audience if they do not react as they had hoped. As always the onus of getting your message across is on you as the communicator.

Beware of handing out visual material during a presentation. If you want your audience to take away with them a visual reminder of what you have said, it is better to keep such material to the end rather than hand it out in the middle of your talk. Interesting brochures, photographs and diagrams can often prove more absorbing than a presenter.

Acceptance of the benefit of your proposals is crucial.

To achieve it tell your audience what your ideas will do for them in their situations as individuals or what your ideas will do for other people in whom your audience are interested, their staff, distributors, superiors, colleagues, customer, shareholders.

The audience wants to know what your ideas will do in terms of what they want done. For example, if they want to be certain that your equipment can easily be operated by semi-skilled labour, it is time-wasting to emphasise that it fits into a small space thereby increasing production per square foot. Therefore, if you want your proposals to be desirable to your audience, select the results and benefits they will get that relate to their need, arranging the sequence so that one result logically leads to another until eventually all their needs are met.

Validity

Validity of your points may be questioned, albeit mentally, by your audience, especially if your proposals are new to them. Examples can be substantiated by quoting specific situations where they have worked. When quoting these examples, or when referring to third parties who have adopted your ideas:

- don't start with such references; instead, use them to support claims you have already made
- ensure that the company or people to whom you refer are respected by the audience
- ensure that the circumstances in both cases are sufficiently similar to make your point acceptable
- tell your audience the desirable results the third party obtained
- gain agreement from the third party that you can quote their results.

Agreement

Agreement on the part of your audience if not always visible. Blank silence can imply agreement, disagreement, bewilderment or boredom. You need agreement on each point before moving on the next one. It is useful to check it by constant observation of their facial expressions and by asking questions if their facial expressions create doubt, for example, 'Are you satisfied that you will have a quality image by using this design?'

Objective 3: To maintain attention

In many presentations the middle is the part least remembered, the part where attention is lost, where credibility falls, where objections arise and where rejection sets in. If the beginning has been good, the middle should be even better.

- Keep telling them what your ideas mean to them.
- Keep their eyes occupied by using visual aids, demonstrations, etc.
- Where possible give them something to do.
- Quote examples, stories, etc.
- Maintain your enthusiasm.
- Involve them where possible.

Objective 4: To prevent or handle objections

In formal presentations the audience is just as likely to think of objections as an individual would in a face-to-face situation. The main difference is that objections are less frequently voiced in formal presentations. It is therefore important that possible objections are considered in advance by the presenter and the answers incorporated into the presentation. For example: 'Of course the initial cost is high, but all the evidence shows that the return far exceeds that of other methods. For example . . .'

If objections are voiced, the objectors want their views acknowledged by the presenter and answered sympathetically. It pays the presenter to handle objections in the following ways:

- Pausing – this give them time to think and prevents the temptation to crush the objector with a snappy rebuttal and potential put down, which will inevitably alienate the individual.
- Acknowledging that the objector has a point, for example: 'Yes, that is an important consideration.'
- Answering by concentrating on what the objector wants.
- Wherever possible seeking assurance from objectors that you have resolved the objection to their satisfaction.
- If the objection is unclear, clarify it by getting objectors to explain what they mean.

Conducting the presentation: the ending

No matter how long a presentation has lasted, no matter what the subject is, the audience expects it to end on a high note. If it has been good at the beginning and better in the middle, it deserves to be best at the end. If it has been a battle, this is your last chance to make a good impression.

The end is where all the threads need to be joined together and all your presentational skills combined to produce a climax that leaves the audience impressed, convinced, and eager to commit to your proposals.

The psychological barrier

Many speakers feel uncomfortable at having to conclude a presentation. They fight shy of asking for a commitment. Yet a commitment is what they want. They fight shy because they are afraid of getting a rejection and they prefer to leave things open. Such an attitude is understandable, but weak. The audience expects the presenter to draw conclusions from the presentation. The presenter should confidently ask for a commitment because a commitment is in the audience's interest as well as in the presenter's.

How to conclude a presentation

There are several techniques for this, but in every presentation the presenter should be concentrating on the needs of the audience when winding up, so that their minds are being focused on their objectives rather than on the presenter's.

From a structural point of view it helps:

- to refer back to the theme – audience needs
- to summarise the points you have made
- if presenting a plan of action, to state it in a structured sequence. Don't leave the audience with a bundle of generalities.

Asking for a commitment can be done by using one or more of the following methods:

- **Direct request**

  'Can we take it then that you will want to go ahead?'

- **Command**

  'Take my advice, adopt this campaign, and let the sales pour in.'

- **Alternatives**

  'As you have seen, your problem can be solved by a comprehensive plan which will be ready in three months or by a gradual process starting now and phased over six months. Do you prefer to start now or wait for the comprehensive plan to be ready?'

- **Immediate gain from immediate decision**

  'As you know, your competitors have been ominously quiet during the past year and it is believed that they are about to launch a similar product

at any time. To protect your share of the market, I suggest you start the campaign now and make things as difficult for them as possible.'

- **Summary**

  'You want equipment which will reduce your production costs by a minimum of ten per cent. It must be compatible with the equipment you wish to retain and must be fully operational within six weeks from your order being placed. Taking all these points into consideration your best approach will be to purchase our equipment because it will give you what you want.'

Conclusion

The end of a presentation should appear to be a logical development from what has previously been said.

Asking for a commitment from the audience does not mean that a favourable one will be forthcoming. Action will only result if the rest of the presentation has been audience-orientated all the way through. A rough check of its audience orientation is to note the number of times 'you' and 'your' are used compared with 'I', 'we' and 'our'. To ensure that your message gets across, remember:

- **Tell them what you're going to tell them.**
- **Tell them.**
- **Then tell them what you've told them.**

PRESENTER'S CHECKLIST

The title of my presentation is _____

The aim of my presentation is _____

_____

Who am I talking to? _____

What are their *needs*? _____

Opening words? (how am I going to gain their attention?) _____

Middle? (how am I going to maintain their interest? do I need charts/props?)

_____

_____

_____

Prevent objections? (what objections will there be; how will I identify, acknowledge, handle/answer?)_____

_____

_____

Close? (how will I end my talk?) _____

By summarising? _____

By a story? _____

By three-step formula?_____

By asking for action? _____

By assigning a task? _____

By alternatives? _____

_____

_____

Remember to:
- smile
- keep eye contact with your audience
- start well, get better as you end
- end on a high note
- write your talk as a checklist
- keep your visuals simple.

Presenter's dos and don'ts

Do...

- present well-groomed appearance
- dress appropriately
- look like an expert
- get your back to wall or curtain
- be yourself
- write your talk as checklist
- smile from time to time
- talk louder than normal
- keep eye contact
- face your audience
- stand erect
- stand slightly on your toes
- lean forward a little
- leave your spectacles on or off
- use variety of gestures
- tell them what you are going to tell them
- then tell them
- end by telling them what you told them
- get a good ending
- remove visuals when they have served their purpose
- finish before you are expected to.

Don't...

- write your talk as an essay
- read your talk
- talk to your notes
- have distractions behind you
- talk to your visuals
- talk to the blackboard
- walk up and down
- lean on the lectern
- fidget with yourself
- play with your clothes
- use the same gesture continually
- compete with distractions
- compete with your own material: if you pass an item out to be looked at stop talking till it has been examined by all
- stand in front of a window
- wear clothes that distract attention from what you are saying
- fidget with your notes
- overrun your allotted time
- smoke.

The use of visual aids

The range of visual aids is large and continues to grow in both size and complexity. This presents you with growing opportunities to improve your meetings and particularly presentations. The selection and use of visual aids should be decided by the needs of the audience and subject. Well used and well prepared visual aids always give an impression of care and forethought by the presenter. Certain points should always be born in mind:

Never forget that your most important visual aid is *yourself*. You are the target of all eyes during the presentation and are standing in plain view at all times. The audience have ample opportunity to study your clothes, your image and posture, etc. You should be turned out in such a way that you add impact and credibility to both yourself and the presentation.

It is better to use no visual aids at all in some instances, than to use them incorrectly. There is nothing more likely to decrease the presenter's credibility than an overhead projector slide shining on the ceiling or a film operated at double speed.

Presenters should be sufficiently conversant with the apparatus to ensure that they can concentrate on the message being put across and not on operating the overhead projector, etc.

Applications and techniques of visual aids

Visual aid	Advantages	Disadvantages	Applications	Guide to use
Flip charts	Versatile Flexible Can refer back Can be prepared in advance Clean and fresh Easy to transport	Oversized jotting pad. Turning away from audience to write can break contact.	Key words, headings, diagrams The build up of a simple visual message, particularly when talking informally to a small group of people. The display of prominent back-ground information during the presentation. Flip chart sequences can be used to build up an increasing mine of information, so revealing the successive stages of a story.	Use simple illustrations only. If a complicated drawing has to be involved, draw a faint outline on the board before-hand. Practise writing quickly and clearly. Hold the pen like a brush. Write in capital letters. Do not talk to the flip chart.
Whiteboard	Flexibility Versatility Projection screen Magnetic board	Difficult to keep clean. Bulky to transport.	Key words, headings, diagrams The build up of a simple visual message, particularly when talking informally to a small group of people. The display of prominent background information dur-ing the presentation.	Illustrations – use simple illustrations only. If a compli-cated drawing has to be involves, draw a faint outline on the board beforehand. Practise writing quickly and clearly. Hold the pen like a brush.

Visual aid	Advantages	Disadvantages	Applications	Guide to use
Magnetic	Good impact Good for large groups Ready-prepared aids Projection screen White board Visuals can be added moved or removed at will.	Heavy to transport. Frequent replacement of visuals necessary.	Large audience where flexibility of display items is required.	Check location Check sequence Ensure they work
Velcro on felt board	Very portable Presentational advantages of magnetic board Inexpensive Good impact Will take any light-weight material.	Aids could get dog-eared. Inflexible, cannot be used without ready-prepared aids. Aids can drop off unless they are kept very light.	Large audience where flexibility of display items is required.	Ensure they work. Prepare the sequence first.
Computer display and multimedia equipment	High resolution Colour Sound Linked into own lap-top computer Flexibility Control	Initial capital outlay. Expensive to hire.	Particularly useful for large groups or business presentations.	Practise techniques. Not for the enthusiastic amateur.
Smart boards	All the advantages and disadvantages of the computer and multimedia equipment but with board touch control can be linked to any computer network			

Visual aid	Advantages	Disadvantages	Applications	Guide to use
Slide projector	Photographs are always authentic Visual attraction Professional impact Easily available Details can be magnified	Room has to be blacked-out. Projector has to be placed in the body of the meeting to get necessary projector throw where it can be a distraction. There are eight different ways of inserting a slide – only one is correct. Slides are easily damaged or lost.	To show pictorial material about people, places and objects, when you need to show real photographs. When you have photographs you can easily obtain relevant slides.	Use a magazine – slides can then be loaded beforehand to be shown in the correct sequence. Use an extension control lead which also means that you can refocus the picture as required. Arrange cues for timing and raising of main lights. Stand well clear of screen when using a pointer. Use a laser pointer. Remember to face the audience again before speaking. Put your slide transparencies in glass mounts. It is expensive but the only sure way of protection from dust and grease. Store slides in magazine between presentations.

Visual aid	Advantages	Disadvantages	Applications	Guide to use
Overhead projector	Speaker faces audience throughout presentation. No darkening of room necessary. If screen is positioned correctly behind speaker, nothing can obscure it. Anything transparent can be projected. Related positions of transparencies on the plate can be used to build up a picture, adding life and movement to a presentation. Parts of transparencies can be masked and the content revealed as the session progresses. Shapes, models and cutlays can be placed on the projector and moved around, as with magnetic and flannel boards.	Projection system reduces size of lettering on screen, small lettering may become unreadable. The main disadvantage of the overhead projector is that because of its versatility and ease of use it is also the easiest visual aid to use badly.	Combines applications for all other visual aids.	Switch off when the aid is not being used or when changing overlays. Remember to write carefully and clearly, pointing whenever possible. Try to avoid typed transparencies. Keep the roll clean and change it frequently. Always have a spare bulb at hand. Place prepared transparencies carefully to avoid angle shadow. Fit screen size to audience and room size.

Visual aid	Advantages	Disadvantages	Applications	Guide to use
Video/tape recorder	Flexible True reproduction Instant replay facility Easy to update contents Realistic	Expensive to buy or hire Bulky to transport Limited use for large group unless large screen available. Can lose audiences attention if too long.	Rehearsal for important presentations. Must relate to subject matter with no padding.	A high standard is expected on the TV screen. Practise techniques continually to achieve good quality presentation.

Activity 12

Using visual aids

1 Identify those visual aids with which you have not had first hand experience.

2 Prepare and implement an action plan to gain the relevant practical experience.

Activity 13

Presentation checklists

1 Prepare a group presentation evaluation checklist.

2 Evaluate three past or present group presentations using the above checklist.

SECTION 3

Managing and developing your sales area

Monitoring and forecasting sales performance

Planning

The first stage in the selling process, and one that cannot be over-emphasised, is often the cause of many lost sales. Many salespeople fail to pay sufficient attention and give real commitment to planning, and rely too much on experience.

Experience is likely to be a dangerous teacher simply because what happened in the past is not always likely to fit the present or the future. Ten years so-called experience can often be ten times one year doing the same thing – *not always learning from past mistakes*.

In order to plan both effectively and efficiently, it is necessary to establish procedures to monitor, gather and record all vital information that is relevant to your selling activities.

Forecasting is an integral part and a key stage in the salesperson's planning process. Having the facts and determining likely trends play a major part in planning your required level of sale activity, thereby increasing the likelihood of meeting many of your buyer's and company's needs.

Sales activity

Focusing purely on sales results against target generates either euphoria or depression and in reality there is nothing that you can do about results.

There is an old saying 'Look after the pennies and the pounds will look after themselves'. So it is in selling. Identify all the quantifiable activities that you have to perform before the sale is completed.

Results stem from activity or lack of it! Results cannot be changed but activities can, both in quality and in quantity.

SAMPLE ACTIVITY RECORDING FORM

Week No	Calls		Interviews		Prospect calls		Enquiries		Orders		Value of order	
	Week	Year to Date	Week	Year to Date	Week	Year to Date	Week	Year to Date	Week	Year to Date	Week	Year to Date

Key activities

Identify the measurable items of business-generating activity, e.g.

- Number of calls made to existing customers.
- Number of calls made to potential customers.
- Number of new customers.
- Number of proposals raised.
- Number of demonstrations carried out.
- Number of customers lost.
- Number of enquiries.

Once the key business activity is monitored, key priorities can then be established, by establishing key averages and ratios, for example:

- Average number of calls per day/week to existing customers.
- Average number of potential customer calls made per day/week.
- Average number of customers lost per week.
- Ratio of new accounts to prospective calls.
- Ratio of proposals to calls made.
- Ratio of demonstrations to proposals.

As an example let us assume a situation where the object of a sales call is to obtain an enquiry which then generates a firm quotation. The product is such that a demonstration is the next objective, from which it is hoped to generate an order. Between each of these stages to the final order, operating ratios exist. Based on historical experience it would be known that:

- one enquiry/quotation results from every four calls (Ratio 1 : 4)
- one demonstration results from every three quotations (Ratio 1 : 3)
- one order results from every two demonstrations (Ratio 1 : 2)

In this example 24 calls would be needed to produce one order and, unless the average order value is high, this would be an unacceptable ratio.

Recording activity in this way clearly indicates to the salesperson where the effort and skill development needs to be concentrated. If preferred, ratios can be expressed in percentage terms.

A sample sales activity recording form is shown opposite.

Sales trends

Regardless of how your results are targeted – product volume, sterling value, leads, etc. – as a salesperson you have at your fingertips a wealth of vital information that can support your planning and influence subsequent results. For example: record quantifiable results by customer, not only as they occur, but on a rolling basis, for example, year to date and year on year.

Extending this across your total customer base will indicate clear trends and it will also enable you to identify where to focus future short- and long-term strategy. Recording actual turnover by customer and groups of customers or sales territory, will enable you to produce valuable information that takes much of the 'crystal ball gazing' out of planning.

Typical information to calculate:

- Average order value – by trade sector or by specific area.
- Average frequency of ordering – decreasing or increasing.
- Where does 80 per cent of your business come from? (*Pareto Principle*)

The Pareto Principle:

In the distribution of economic activity in a market, a large proportion of the activity is often accounted for by a small number of market operators. The ratio is often 80:20, i.e. 20% of the accounts produce 80% of the revenue.

Such information is necessary if you are to plan the successful development of your sales area. The above information will tell you:

- how many customers you need
- the frequency of contact
- how many new customers you need
- where to focus your activity.

Without this information planning the development of your territory is difficult, a subject to be discussed later in this handbook.

Moving Annual Totals/Averages

Seasonal trends, promotional activity and holidays can, and often will, distort annual results. A way to smooth out these factors and further enhance planning and trend analysis is known as Moving Annual Totals. Take the preceding twelve months performance up to and including the month in question. At each month end, add that month's figures and deduct the corresponding month from the previous year. This will indicate present performance compared with the same period in the previous year. Dividing the total by twelve can also give you the Moving Monthly Average.

A significant benefit in Moving Annual Totals and Averages, is that in the main they will never swing dramatically, but a movement over three months could indicate a clear trend. See page 126.

Many software packages have the facilities for producing this kind of information providing a further valuable tool in forecasting sales performance.

Colleagues'/competitors' sales

Although volumes and key operating activities may sometimes be difficult to obtain accurately, talking to the trade and competitors' sales representatives may shed some light, enabling you to draw some comparisons with your own performance. Maintain detailed records of all information you glean from whatever source. Odd pieces of information can often be added together to form a clear picture.

Market conditions in relation to sales performance

The degree of detail required to analyse one's own performance, will obviously vary among industries and companies. However, some level of market analysis is extremely useful in planning your own sales activity. The example shown on page 127 can be extended into product groups, trade sectors or areas as the need dictates, and is a further step in forecasting sales performance.

MOVING ANNUAL TOTAL AND MOVING MONTHLY AVERAGE

Month	Total	M.A.T.	M.M.A.
January 1993	10,000		
February	20,000		
March	20,000		
April	30,000		
May	30,000		
June	20,000		
July	40,000		
August	30,000		
September	30,000		
October	30,000		
November	10,000		
December	10,000	280,000	23,333
January 1994	20,000	290,000	24,167
February	20,000	290,000	24,167
March	30,000	300,000	25,000
April	50,000	320,000	26,667
May	30,000	320,000	26,667
June	10,000	310,000	25,833
July	40,000	310,000	25,833
August	20,000	300,000	25,000
September	30,500	300,500	25,042
October	30,500	301,000	25,083
November	11,000	302,000	25,167
December	10,500	302,500	25,208
January 1995	22,000	304,500	25,375
February	23,000	307,500	25,625
March	35,000	312,500	26,042
April	52,000	314,500	26,208

SALES PERFORMANCE ANALYSIS

Last year	This year	Forecast next year
		Market
		% Change over previous year
		Actual sales
		% Change over previous year
		Market share

Activity 14

Identifying your key sales activities, ratios and averages

1 List all the sales generating activities that are relevant to your job.

_____

_____

_____

_____

_____

_____

2 List the key operating ratios that are critical.

_____

_____

_____

_____

_____

_____

3 Design a form, either manual or electronic, for recording key activities incorporating year to date figures.

How to prepare a territory sales plan

Look at any successful company or, indeed, individual and you will find that planning has a continuing and major part to play in that success. The likelihood of any company or individual surviving without a plan is almost nil. Far from constraining flexibility and minimising opportunities, planning allows time to adapt to changing circumstances in a controlled way, thus ensuring that as and when opportunities arise, they may be capitalised upon. Planning is not a one-off activity, it is a dynamic process concerned with looking ahead in order to decide the appropriate channels through which resources can be directed towards the attainment of objectives.

A sales plan is a working document and therefore needs to be continually revised and evaluated against actual results and changing circumstances. As with any sound plan, instead of merely predicting the future, a well structured and researched sales plan sets out to influence it.

Before reviewing the structure and process of developing a territory sales plan, it is relevant and important to consider why many people fail in planning. Clearly, negative attitudes play a major part in determining the cause of failure and to some extent even fear – the fear of having to make long term commitments. People attempt to hide this fear with excuses such as 'I have not got time to plan' and are much more comfortable criticising other people's plans after the event.

Among the most common but important reasons for ineffective planning are:

- lack of commitment to planning
- confusion of planning studies with plans
- failure to see planning as a rational process
- lack of clearly defined quantitative aims, goals, objectives
- excessive reliance on experience
- resistance to change
- seeing plans as constricting and inflexible
- fear of failure

- not knowing how to develop a territory sales plan and unable to acknowledge this.

How does the territory sales plan fit into the company's corporate plan?

The directors of a company will agree its corporate goals. These are normally expressed in financial terms and will define what the company aims to achieve within specific time frames. These will be in clear and precise terms of from one to three years and in broader terms for subsequent years, all of which will be reviewed and updated on an annual basis.

The corporate goals will embrace sales revenue, return on capital, profit before tax and other key corporate aims that may be crucial to the future of the company. Once the corporate goals are established, the whole planning process can begin by establishing objectives and strategies. Objectives are what is to be achieved. Strategies are how we intend to get there.

Having established the corporate goals, these will be reflected in the company plan in terms of corporate objectives and strategies. In their turn, these will be passed down the line to each functional operation:

- Production
- Finance
- Distribution
- Personnel
- Purchasing
- Marketing and Sales.

Each operation will be asked to prepare its own plan, incorporating specific objectives and strategies that are compatible with each function within the company.

Marketing and Sales, although two distinct functions, will work closely together on the basis that *Marketing conceives and Sales implements.*

There may well be circumstances where you will be asked to submit your own territory targets or to evaluate draft targets prior to ratification. In both these situations you will be involved in a further discipline – forecasting. Although this is a vast subject in itself, sales forecasting is not so difficult as much of the basic information required is available and if presented in the right way it will enable you to make reasonable forecasts based on facts rather than pure guesswork.

For obvious reasons the Marketing and Sales plan has a major bearing on almost all other departments within the company, that is, Production, Purchasing, Plant and Resources, Personnel and Finance.

A territory sales plan, indeed any plan, must address and answer the following questions:

- **Where are you now?** Analysing the situation.
- **Where are you going?** Establishing goals, aims, objectives.
- **How will you get there?** Strategy, implementation.
- **How will it be managed?** Monitoring, control.

Where are you now?

Before any clear objectives and strategies can be established and implementation plans agreed, it is vital to establish where your territory stands at the moment. As when starting out on any journey, before deciding the best route to take, you must know not only your destination, but where you are starting from.

The difference between what you want to achieve and what you will achieve if you continue doing the same things, is often referred to as the *planning gap*:

What you want to achieve – Results at current rate = Planning gap

SWOT analysis

A classical and effective way used by organisations and marketing departments is to conduct a SWOT analysis: **S**trengths and **W**eaknesses as they relate to **O**pportunities and **T**hreats in the market place.

The strengths and weaknesses relate to internal factors, that is, the company and its products. Opportunities and threats are inevitably external factors over which the company has no direct control. Conducting an honest SWOT analysis of your territory, will indicate where your objectives and strategies must be focused.

It should be borne in mind that something that may be a strength may also be a potential weakness. For example, you may have a long-established nucleus of loyal customers on whom you focus most of your efforts (strength). However, the market and distribution patterns may be changing in favour of other suppliers and you may have failed to recognize this trend (weakness).

Example of a territory SWOT analysis

Strengths	Weaknesses
• Well established product • Long established customer base • Sound relationship with most customers	• Number of customers declining • Insufficient new customers to compensate • Lack of localised marketing activity • Lack of time to prospect for new business
Opportunities	**Threats**
• Develop new markets • Increase product range in existing customers	• Increased local competitor activity • Increased activity from overseas competitors

Having completed your territory SWOT analysis, you then need to convert this knowledge into positive objectives and ask yourself for:

- **Strengths** – What can be done to capitalise on each strength? That is, How can I use this to my advantage?

- **Weaknesses** – What can be done to overcome or limit the effect of each weakness?

- **Opportunities** – What can be done to take the most advantage from each opportunity?

- **Threats** – How can the effect of each threat be minimised or removed? Can the threats be turned into opportunities?

At this stage you are beginning to see the basis of your plan – the key objectives and strategies required.

Activity analysis

There is an indisputable link between sales revenue and the level of sales activity, therefore, it makes sound sense to consider carefully, what are the key stages in the sales process and what are the relevant ratios and averages. By careful analysis of your past activity levels and with relevant calculations, you will be able to incorporate quite specific activity targets into your sales plan. The time periods over which you review your actual activity against those set will depend on the nature of your business. The ideal is weekly but certainly no longer than every four weeks. The ramifications can be serious and even irreversible if several weeks elapse before evaluations are carried out.

Typical information that may be required to analyse your area:

- Results v target – last three years.
- Average sales per customer – last three years.
- Average order value.
- Number of customers who generate 80 per cent of your business.
- Number of live accounts.
- Number of lost accounts and why.
- Number of new accounts.
- Number of accounts with significant potential.
- Average number of calls per week.
- Order to call ratio.
- Ratio of new accounts to prospect calls.
- Competitor activity: to what extent are they becoming more active in your accounts and why?

Wherever possible compare each set of figures over at least the last two to three years. This will give some indication of likely trends. The

Moving Annual Totals and Moving Monthly Averages referred to on page 125, are a first class way of identifying trends and a significant aid to forecasting. For those with access to personal computers, there are many software packages that will calculate Moving Annual Totals and convert them into graphs.

Personal strengths and weaknesses

Your own strengths and weaknesses must also be considered when drawing up your sales plan. Careful and honest thought needs to be given, regarding any aspect of your own attitude, knowledge or skills. Ask yourself:

- *Where do I need to improve my product or company knowledge?*
- *Am I fully conversant with all the company procedures and policies?*
- *Do I need to restructure my journey plan?*
- *Am I fully developing my area?*
- *Am I close enough to my major accounts?*
- *Am I aware of the accounts with potential?*
- *What aspects of my selling skills need improving?*

Asking these questions is a strength and reflects the right attitude. Review these points with your manager or a third party and where action is to be taken, incorporate this into your sales plan.

Where are you going?

Throughout the sales plan, you will be defining what you want to achieve: setting objectives, aims, goals and targets. Whatever terms are used there are fundamental but golden rules to apply. They must be both qualitative and quantitative, as one of these qualities without the other will have little if any merit. Adopt the SMART yardstick:

S – Specific
M – Measurable
A – Achievable
R – Realistic
T – Time-bound

Unless each aim, goal or target passes the SMART test, is it of any worth to you or your company? Probably not.

How will it be managed?

However well thought through a plan might be, it is open to failure if one basic element is omitted – control. Control is the process of monitoring activities and events and comparing what is actually happening with what should be happening according to your plan. It is then possible to take corrective action where required, to ensure that objectives are attained on time.

Be quite specific in your plan about what controls you intend to use and, where relevant, who will be involved. The feedback loop of management control is a useful model on which to base your control process element.

Control sequence

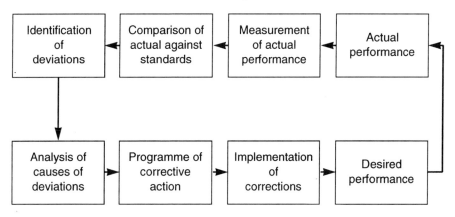

Major accounts

In any sales area there will be a number of large customers whose sales contribution is significant to the area revenue. This is often referred to as the Pareto Principle – 20 per cent of the accounts producing 80 per cent of the revenue. It therefore makes considerable sense when developing your area plan to prepare individual strategies for each of these accounts. You may also wish to consider a similar approach for those customers where there is significant potential. When analysing your business with major accounts, compare your revenue as a percentage against the customers'. Although you may have increased your sales to a customer by 5 per cent their sales of that product may have shown a greater increase so in real terms you are losing business.

Activity 15

SWOT analysis

Complete a SWOT analysis and action plan for your sales area.

Activity 16

'Hit list' targeting

1 List the top ten accounts in your area and by account identify:

   a business by product for the last three years

   b forecast for next year

   c opportunities to introduce new products.

   Prepare a strategy for each account.

2 Identify ten customers with significant potential. Prepare individual strategies.

3 Identify ten potential new customers. Prepare individual strategies.

4a Analyse key sales activity, ratios and averages for the previous two years.

   b Agree future activity levels with your manager.

   c Design a format for recording activity incorporating a year to date figure.

You may use the form given on the next page.

KEY ACCOUNT CUSTOMER STRATEGY FORM

Customer name: _____

Address: _____

_____

Telephone: _____   Fax: _____

Key personnel

Name: _____   Position: _____

Principle buying motives _____

Terms_____

Products stocked_____

Competitors products stocked_____

Sales results by product

	199_		199_		199_	
Product	Actual	Forecast	Actual	Forecast	Actual	Forecast

199_   Target, Strategy, Action plan, Review plan – to be agreed
          with customer (give details)

_____

_____

_____

Activity 17

Activity analysis

1 Identify your top ten accounts.

a Analyse what percentage of your total area review do they individually and collectively produce.

b Evaluate the gross profit contribution on the same basis.

c Produce a three year trend analysis and write a summary of the results.

d In each case compare your results with the customer's results for each product and prepare a written summary.

e Based on current trends and marketing activity prepare twelve month forecasts.

2 List the main aims for your area for the next twelve months. Explain the rationale for these aims.

3 Identify your main self-development aims for the next twelve months and explain how you intend to approach them.

4 Identify at least six accounts with significant growth potential. Summarise by account any strategy you intend to adopt. State:

a what support you will require and why

b when you intend to begin

c what your initial action will be

d when you anticipate taking the initial order.

Estimate potential.

Developing a strategy and plan for new business

Why?

There are few commercial environments where the customer base is totally stable and a company is not looking for growth.

It is also a fact that there is, for whatever reason, a 3.5–5 per cent annual shrinkage in a company's customer base.

Consequently a certain number of new customers are required each year to maintain current results.

Therefore, if growth is required, the number of new customers must be in addition to those required to stand still.

How?

There are only two ways in which salespeople can develop their sales revenue:

- Maximise the business through existing customers.
- Develop new customers.

Attitudes play a big part in the whole process of developing new business. To some prospecting is a natural talent, to most it is an acquired skill and to the remainder it is a series of excuses ('I do not have the time').

As with most business functions, without a clear strategy and implementation plan the likelihood of developing new business is almost nil.

Developing a strategy

Stage 1: Analyse business trends in your area, through:

- trade papers/magazines
- marketing information

- customer information
- trade associations
- company sales personnel
- spread and location of your customer base.

Compare information with your own actual performance.

Identify areas where there are new business opportunities.

Stage 2: Decide what are to be your new business aims for the next twelve months:

- number of new customers
- location
- projected first year's revenue.

Stage 3: Identify target prospects and location.

Conduct research into:

- current suppliers
- buying points
- decision-maker or process for new suppliers
- point of contact
- company brochure.

If off your territory discuss joint strategy with colleague.

Stage 4: Integrate into journey plan

Do not allocate days a month for prospecting. This sounds impressive but will rarely happen as days will get used up for so-called problem solving. It is also not a sound use of time and it does not encourage area-wide development.

Making the first call on a prospective customer

The sales sequence is the same, but the emphasis is notably different: even more thought needs to be given to planning and preparation.

Planning and preparation

- *What do you need to know about the prospect in order to make a positive sales proposal?*
- *What have you established and concluded from your research?*
- *What do you need to find out on your first call?*
- *What questions do you need to ask in order to obtain this information?*
- *How do you justify the customer's time and requirement to respond to the questions?*
- *What visual sales aids might you need?*
- *What product samples might you need?*
- *What objections are likely to be raised?*
- *How can you either pre-empt them or respond with sound positive answers?*
- *Have you established who is the decision-maker for authorising a new supplier?*
- *When are they available? Do you need an appointment?*
- *Have they dealt with your company before? If they have why have they ceased dealing with you?*
- *What objectives will you set for the first call?*

Objectives

These will clearly depend on your answers to many of the above questions. Remember that there are many instances where gaining an order on the first call is most unlikely. How can you sell something to people when you do not know what are their precise needs.

Gaining the interview

If you can walk straight in and see the decision-maker, that is one less problem you have to face. If, as in many cases, an appointment is required, this is the first stage in the whole approach to gaining a new customer.

You need to convince the decision-maker that their time with you will not be wasted. However, avoid selling over the telephone. Telephone selling is a specialised skill and best left to the experts.

Consider the decision-maker:

- Busy person, has a business to run.
- Satisfied with current supplier.
- Constantly pestered by salespeople.

Getting in to see prospects is not as difficult as some people make it. Most of the difficulties are only in the mind of the salesperson who tends to imagine difficulties where none exist.

Failing to consider all these points results in a reception full of miscellaneous brochures and business cards left by salespeople convinced that they have made a prospect call or salespeople trying to sell their product over the phone and sending brochures in the post, which inevitably end up in the bin. But again convinced that they have made an attempt at prospecting.

Introduction

Having gained the appointment you come face to face with the potential customer. Before you arrive and in those seconds when making the formal introductions, what is going through the person's mind? They will often be guarded, thinking some if not all of the following:

'I don't know who you are'.
'I don't know your company'.
'I don't know your company's product'.
'I don't know what your company stands for'.
'I don't know your company's customers'.
'I don't know your company's record'.
'I don't know your company's reputation'.
'Now! What was it you wanted to tell me?'

Your opening statement could well influence the whole quality of the interview and any future successful outcome. Remember, you have one chance to make a good first impression.

Your opening statement, in probably no more than 30 seconds, must achieve the following:

- **Attention** – sound positive.
- **Interest** – create genuine interest.

- **Desire** – to hear more.
- **Action** – prepared to respond to your questions.

Do not start making a presentation in your opening statement.

The main criticism from most buyers throughout industry, is that too many salespeople do not find out what the customer wants: do that and you will gain instant respect. Ask customers to clarify some points, in order that you may fine-tune your presentation to meet their needs – then into your presentation.

Self-induced adverse conditions:

- Conveying lack of confidence.
- Not addressing person by name.
- Talking too quickly or too slowly.
- Fumbling with briefcase.
- Using weak/insulting sentences.
  '... passing by'
  'just popped in ...'
- Being apologetic.
  'Hope I'm not troubling you'.
  'Forgive me for intruding'.
  'Sorry I ...'

Close

If the intention is to see the prospect a second time, make the appointment there and then. Do not offer to contact them later.

Writing for an appointment

There are some instances where it will be necessary to write requesting an appointment. The content and quality of your letter will need to achieve the same as your introductory statement.

- **Attention**
- **Interest**
- **Desire**
- **Action**

How to write such a letter is dealt with in the section Effective Communication.

If you have to write requesting an interview, a follow-up phone call shortly after they receive the letter is crucial.

Telephoning for an appointment

Every time you use the telephone you are selling yourself. The most important thing to remember about the telephone is that most of the time when you use the instrument, you are making or breaking a sale – and the product is *you*.

Before picking up the telephone, you must be conditioned to use it. You must know what company you are going to call, who you are going to speak to, what you are going to say, and have the objective of the telephone call firmly fixed in your mind. You are selling one thing and one thing only – *an appointment*. You should not use the call for anything else – and the last thing you should expect is a decision to buy.

Jerome K Jerome once said, 'I like work – I can sit and look at it for hours'. How often have you gone to the telephone without being prepared – and just looked at it, wondering what to do, who to call, what to say. You then carry out a worthless exercise to justify starting in the first place and, when the desired results have not come, you sit back and look at the telephone again, wondering why you were unsuccessful! We have all done it at some time or another, some of us all too often.

Before picking up the telephone you must be prepared

- You must be comfortable and have a positive mental attitude.
- You must be mentally prepared to communicate, as one business person to another, offering something which might be mutually profitable. Does your mental image of yourself fit this role?
- You must have your prospect cards in front of you, and they must show the correct names and telephone numbers.
- You must decide to whom you wish to speak.

- You must know what you are going to say when you start. (Why not have a typed telephone script in front of you to bring you back on course when the conversation looks as if it might stray from your objective of making an appointment?)
- State briefly that you are telephoning for an appointment.

    'I particularly wish to meet you, so I'm telephoning to find a convenient time. Which would be best, next Tuesday or Thursday?'
- Always have a brief but interesting reason for wanting to meet the prospect, such as:

    'I want to meet you to discuss methods of extending the life of your shovels which could save your company a great deal of money. Which day would be best, Tuesday or Thursday?'
- Anticipate the few objections or questions that might arise and have answers to them.
- Have your diary beside you.

When you speak

- **Smile**. A smile does come through on the telephone. Remember the person cannot see you, but will still form a mental image based on what they hear.
- Modulate your voice pleasantly with your mouth close to the instrument.
- Make sure your voice conveys maturity, enthusiasm, a business-like approach, interest and warmth.
- Speak clearly and precisely and get to the point immediately. Your call should not last much more than 60 seconds. Expect them to say 'yes' and they probably will. **The longer you are on the telephone, the less likely you are able to gain the appointment.**
- Remember your object is to gain an appointment and do not be sidetracked into making a presentation.
- Mention specific times and dates – *always* give two alternatives. Always have your diary at hand.
- Size up the person on the telephone and govern your manner accordingly.
- Remember you are laying the groundwork for a personal call and courtesy is vital.

- Bear in mind that the telephone is your best friend and use it accordingly.
- Develop the habit of closing gently and politely, but positively and repeatedly, always using the alternative method of closing. Always conclude by repeating the agreed time and date.

Don't:

- get anyone else to place the call for you and then keep the person at the other end waiting after the call has been put through.
- shout or whisper.
- forget that *you* make the call, *you* are interrupting their work.
- use technical terms that they might not understand.
- make an appointment with the wrong person – it is always better to wait for the right person.

Very few objections will arise – and almost all of them are common and can be anticipated:

> 'I'm not ready to talk to representatives about that project yet.'
> 'I'm far too busy to see anyone today – this week – this month.'
> 'I'm just off on holiday.'
> 'Write me a letter telling me why you want to see me.'
> 'What's it all about?'
> 'You'll have to speak to Mr X.'
> 'I'm not interested.'

It is always important to spend time formulating good answers to each possible objection.

Remember:

- The prospect is not expecting you to call and has not been trained to resist you – indeed there is no reason why anyone should be – except in the mind of a negative salesperson.
- All the cards are stacked in favour of trained professional salespeople who have thought out their telephone techniques, studied all possible objections and developed good answers to them. You have the initiative and the diary. You have control of the conversation. You have specific objectives. You have belief and enthusiasm. You will get an appointment at least seven out of ten times. No

one, no matter how skilled, can achieve the objective of a telephone call *every time*.

Some answers when 'cold' calling for an appointment

'Sorry, I'm too busy.'	*'Yes, I appreciate that you are a busy man, Mr . . . and that is why I am phoning for an appointment rather than call on the off chance of seeing you.'*
'Send me details.'	*'Certainly I will send you details, Mrs . . . but I would value your personal appraisal on this . . .'*
'Not interested.'	*'I can understand you not being interested in something that you have not had a chance to see, but so that you can judge for yourself . . .'*
'No money – can't afford it.'	*'I can understand you avoiding unnecessary expense and that you have cash flow considerations, however, there is no obligation on your part. All I am asking you to do is to look at this . . . to see whether it will be of value to your company . . .'*
'I have no need.'	*'You may be right, Ms . . . however, many companies are currently using this . . . and finding it most economical/ beneficial . . .'*
'See my supervisor.'	*'Thank you, Mr . . . I shall certainly do that; will you give me his name so that I can contact him at a later date? However, the benefits of this . . . are more appreciated by the person responsible for profit such as yourself . . .'*
'I am satisfied with my present supplier.'	*'Yes, I can appreciate that, Mrs . . . however, there are certain benefits of this . . . which I would like to discuss with you . . .'*
'What's it all about, tell me now.'	*'Miss . . . the benefits of this . . . can be outlined quickly by means of illustration, facts and figures, which would be impossible to explain over the telephone . . .'*
'You are wasting your time.'	*'Mr . . . since this might be of immense value to you and your company, I certainly don't mind spending the time . . .'*
All occasions.	*'I appreciate your point of view Mrs . . ., but I would welcome the opportunity to present the facts/benefits for your appraisal.'*

Activity 18

Activity planning for prospective customers

Evaluate and list:

a   the number of lost customers in last two years.

b   the number of prospect calls made in last twelve months?

c   the number of new customers in last twelve months?

d   the number of calls required before account is opened?

Now you have key ratios and averages that can be used in your activity plan for developing new business.

Activity 19

Introducing your company

Prepare an opening statement that dynamically describes your company. It should last no longer than 30 seconds.

Territory planning and management

Every salesperson has 24 available hours every day. However, that is where the similarity ends. How this time is managed is a further factor in the success equation.

Much attention is given to time management, and rightly so, through the use of personal organisers. But although a valuable tool, it can be counter-productive to a salesperson if not used in conjunction with a well-thought-through, planned and documented territory management system.

Many salespeople's response to journey planning is that they need to be flexible and cannot be constrained by a journey plan. They fail to see that such a system facilitates organised flexibility.

Allowing for holidays, meetings etc., there are on average 220 working days in a year. It has also been calculated that the average salesperson uses only two to three hours of actual selling time per day.

How much time do you spend?

What are the benefits to be derived from territory planning and management?

- Contact with customers at a planned frequency in line with business demands.
- Planned contact with prospective customers.
- Identification of areas where new business is required.
- Optimising face to face selling time.
- Less driving time so less stress.
- Increased number of prospect calls, for example, one more prospective customer seen every day would mean about 220 extra contacts in 12 months.
- More new customers.
- Significant reduction in dashing all over the territory, responding to so-called urgent calls.

> **Reduced sales costs = increased profitable sales**

Territory planning

Territory planning is the strategic arrangement of time and travel whereby a salesperson endeavours to:

1 service existing accounts with no more than the frequency necessary to ensure maximum turnover and maintain goodwill

2 prospect for new business by making 'pioneering' calls

3 maximise selling time under both of the above points, by the economical coverage and development of the territory, to minimise travel time.

Effective territory planning may therefore be defined as the system by which a salesperson balances points 1 and 2 by the systematic practice of point 3. This is achieved by five stages leading to the eventual plan.

Stage 1

Estimate the total number of calls theoretically possible within a given period:

- between existing customers according to their importance (i.e. potential)
- between existing customers and 'prospects'.

To give an example:

If there are 20 selling days per month on average over the year (after allowing for holidays, meetings, etc,) and the average call rate is 6 per day, then the total number of calls per year is $20 \times 12 \times 6 = 1{,}440$ calls.

By deducting, say 10 per cent for 'pioneering' calls (the proportion of time should be agreed with your manager), this determines that 144 calls are devoted to 'prospecting' and 1,296 calls are available to call on existing accounts:

	1,440	total calls available
less	144	'prospecting' calls
leaving	1,296	calls for existing accounts

Stage 2

Place existing customers into categories according to potential. Be realistic and avoid over-calling. For example:

Potential business	Category
over £12000	A
£8000–£12000	B
£5000–£8000	C
Up to £5000	D

Decide the call frequency required to 'service' an account according to its potential. Be mindful that in practice you may have valid reasons to call *less* frequently than the stipulated call rate, but generally it should not be necessary to call *more* frequently than the category warrants. For example:

Category	No. of customers in category	Call frequency	Calls per year
A	24	Once per month	288
B	60	Once every 2 months	360
C	100	Once every 3 months	400
D	150	Once every 6 months	300
			1,348

We established in Stage 1 that, theoretically, 1,296 calls are available against 1,348 needed, so we are 52 short.

Carefully review the categories of customers and consider their call frequencies. Always adjust from the lowest category (with the least potential), on the principle that servicing existing customers in category D must not be at the expense of pioneering calls that will create new business.

Note. 'Servicing' in this context implies obtaining continuous and increasing business from existing customers as well as providing after-sales service.

Therefore it may be necessary to reduce the calls on category D customers or even, as a last resort, omit calling on some of them completely. Consider the extent to which telephone contact would be sufficient.

Stage 3

As far as possible, categorise your prospects into the same A B C D categories as existing customers. This will help you ensure that the call frequency matches their likely importance to your company, that is, their potential.

Stage 4

Mark the location of every customer and prospect you visit on a large scale map. Use a colour code to distinguish the categories and a different type of marker to distinguish customers from prospects.

Unless an area is compact it may be necessary to carry out this stage using separate maps for the large towns in your area.

Stage 5

Having assumed that there are, on average, 20 working days in every month, the objective is to cover the area, not every customer, once in every 20-day cycle in such a way that you visit both customers and prospects with the call frequency previously agreed.

To do this, first divide the territory into five major areas, one for each day of the working week, and within each of these major areas group customers and prospects into four sub-areas so that although you visit the major area once a week, you visit each of the sub-areas within it only once in every twenty days. (See the example opposite.)

In the example given in Stage 2 there are in fact 24 category A customers in this territory, therefore four of the sub-areas will have two A customers each, to be called on once in every monthly cycle. Similarly, there is a total of 60 B customers and this means that 30 of them must be called on in every cycle.

Thus in sub-area 9 there will be several more markers than the six actually shown and, of these, the A customers will be called on every month, the B customers in alternate months, and the C and D customers every three and six months respectively.

The numbering of the 20 sub-areas depends on the location of the salesperson's base. It is assumed, in the example, that this is reason-

Territory planning and management

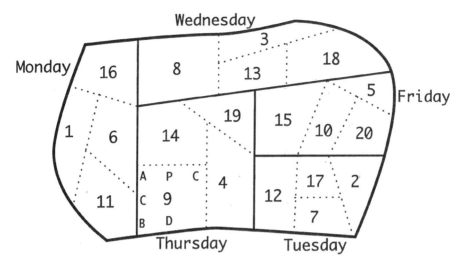

In the diagram, sub-area 9 shows five customer calls and one pioneering call, i.e. the plan for one of the four Thursdays in the monthly cycle.

ably central, so that on alternate days the salesperson will be at opposite ends of the area. The sequence of sub-area numbering is important because it takes care of the need for 'emergency' calls or telephone requests.

With the numbering as shown, a salesperson should always be able to make a special (unscheduled) call within 48 hours, because on the next day but one he or she will always be in the *adjacent* area to where the call is required, thus minimising the deviation required to make the special visit.

By working to this system the salesperson will visit each sector of the territory every week. Consequently, if a call is missed for whatever reason on a Thursday of week two, it can be called on with only a short detour only seven days later on Thursday of week three, without making a special journey across the territory. Similarly if a request to make an unscheduled call comes through from any part of the territory, within 48 hours you will be in close proximity. Very few if any so-called urgent requests to call will require a shorter response when explained via a phone call.

Minimising travel time using the circuit system

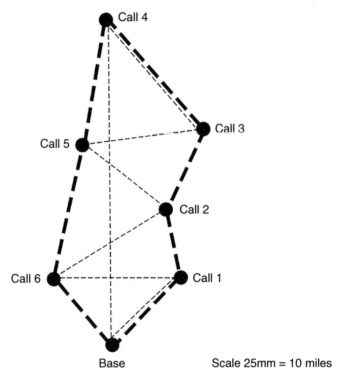

Base
Scale 25mm = 10 miles

Total journey distance

▬ ▬ ▬ Route by the circuit system — 80 miles
- - - - - - - Route by driving out and working back or by working out — 112 miles
and driving back

Circuit system

Even further time can be saved by a logical organisation of the daily
calls. Travelling time can be significantly reduced by adopting the
'Circuit' system. By examining a typical day's calls it will show that
the circuit shape journey plan is the shortest distance between each
call. Compare this approach to the traditional approach – driving to
the furthest point of the territory or call and working back. On an
equal time basis the circuit system will reduce travel time and be
more effective and efficient. It must be recognised that any system
must be mindful of the needs and influencing factors relating to individual situations. The system is flexible and applying some of the elements can and will produce significant benefits.

After completion of your journey plan on a suitable map, the next stage is to complete a journey sheet for each week. A sample journey sheet is given on page 156.

This will aid planning and is far simpler to use than constantly referring to a map. If you use an organiser, it is useful to have the complete set reduced to fit into your organiser. This will enable you to make instant appointments that fit into your territory management system.

This system can be adapted to suit call frequencies other than the ones used as examples. Amend it as necessary to suit your own circumstances.

The basic principles involved have the following advantages:

1 They ensure that the territory is covered systematically and in depth with regard to the geography of the area, and they regulate call frequency to match customer potential.

2 They ensure that enough pioneering calls are mixed in with existing customer calls to make good wastage and promote growth.

3 They provide flexibility to accommodate the need to make special calls in response to telephone requests or enquiries.

> **Plan your work and work your plan.**

Territory content review

Journey plans can never be a permanent system. Customer buying patterns and demands change and consequently call frequency will change. Therefore journey plans need to be reviewed on a regular basis, dependant on your own business, but should be totally reviewed at least every 12 months.

A useful method is to complete a territory content review to establish the mix of accounts and calls. An example is given on page 157.

The left-hand column can reflect areas or even trade sectors as required, but will give an instant picture of your customer mix.

JOURNEY PLAN

Week No.	Month				
	Monday	Tuesday	Wednesday	Thursday	Friday

TERRITORY CONTENT REVIEW

Salesperson _____   Date _____

Area/ Trade sector	'A' Calls		'B' Calls		'C' Calls		'D' Calls		Total A/Cs	Total Calls
	A/Cs	Calls	A/Cs	Calls	A/Cs	Calls	A/Cs	Calls		

Account classification can be adjusted according to potential.

Customer records

Customer record cards

Arrange your record cards according to geographical area relating to your journey plan. Mark each card with the grading in the top right-hand corner and colour code it with colours relating to your map.

The need to maintain customer records, either written or electronic, is clearly obvious. However, the extent of the recorded information needs to be carefully considered. If you accept the principle that knowledge is power, then you can not have too much recorded information on each and every customer. How the information is recorded, stored and updated, is a matter for the individual.

The minimum information should cover the following points:

- Full company name and address, telephone and fax numbers.
- Brief profile of the company.
- Names, initials and titles of all key personnel who are involved with the decision process relating to your product or service and the frequency of contact needed with each person.
- Decision-maker or process.
- Delivery points.
- Service demands/expectations.
- Key buying motives/factors.
- Details of previous calls – points agreed, future points for discussions.
- Where possible, long-term aims and how they see your product or service fitting into these aims.
- How they will measure your product and service.
- Are you a sole supplier or in competition?
- Who are the competitors?
- Frequency of updating the records.

If, in the eyes of customers, you are seen as someone who is really interested in their business, a long-term business relationship is increasingly consolidated.

Activity 20

Journey planning and customer analysis

1 Estimate the average number of calls you can achieve each week and calculate this for 12 months.

2 Calculate the number of selling days available in 12 months. Be mindful of all holidays, meetings, etc.

3 Complete a work state analysis for existing and prospect customers.

4 Complete a journey plan incorporating the circuit system.

5 Record over four weeks, how much time you actually spend selling.

6 Draw conclusions.

7 Prepare action plan to resolve any problems.

Customer service

Much has been written under the banner of customer care and service, but what does it mean? Is it price? Is it delivery? Is it after-sales service? Is it payment terms? Is it promotional support? Is it problem solving? Yes, it may be some or all of these factors.

Service

Time and time again you hear the comment 'We offer good service'. You or your company may well claim to offer good service, but what does the customer think? Service must begin and end with the customer. *You* may consider that you offer and give good service – whatever that means – but have you asked the customer how they will measure service?

Ask the question and carefully record the responses. This will enable you to review on a regular basis your actual performance against the customer's requirements and to take any remedial action that may be needed. This single ongoing act signals clear intent and commitment to meet the customer's service requirements wherever possible.

What is service?

At various times most people give the impression that they are experts on service, particularly when they are on the receiving end of what they consider to be poor service. We all recognise good and poor service when we see it and feel it.

In many instances and situations, quite often it is not the problem itself that causes a customer to seek alternative sources of supply. What is remembered is the way the problem was dealt with.

Whatever form of customer records you keep, ensure that you list in detail the individual service criteria for each customer.

Poor service occurs when people do not get what they expect. This quickly generates emotional reactions of anger, disappointment and a sense of being let down.

Good service occurs when people get at least what they expect and even a little more. This gives people a good feeling and encourages them to repeat the experience.

As salespeople we are in the vanguard of managing and orchestrating customer care and service. Much can be done by the salesperson to show how much genuine commitment you and your company give to this vital area rather than paying it mere lip service:

- Always remember that customers are indispensable to your business.
- Find out exactly what level of service the customer expects and make sure you can meet it.
- Regularly check with each customer the actual service against expectations.
- Ensure that your behaviour shows them that you value them and their business.
- Listen and really hear what the customers are saying and try to understand their point of view.
- Do not commit yourself to things that you cannot fulfil.
- Develop trust in your customer relationships. Honesty is the best policy.
- Treat all complaints seriously, ensure that they are dealt with immediately. Keep the customer informed at all times. 'Passed to the office' is not dealing with the problem, it is abdication.
- Record and analyse complaints for subsequent discussion as a way of improving customer service.
- Problems dealt with effectively and efficiently to the customer's satisfaction, can cement long-term relationships.
- Deliveries on time, to the right place, in the right condition, to the right person.

By reviewing these points on a regular basis, any problems can be brought to the surface and turned into positive action.

At least 50 per cent of all lost business is due to poor service, either the lack of it, or the customer not being convinced that the supplier can meet their expectations – not to price as many believe.

Ask the question 'In addition to a competitive price, what are the critical factors that will influence your decision?' Listen and take notes. If they respond 'Good service', do not assume. Ask 'What service aspects are important?'. Listen and write them down. When they have finished, prompt if you feel that there are some added elements that you can provide.

For example:

> 'What about . . .?'
> 'How important is . . .?'

Then play the whole list back to them. That means you are starting the closing process.

Quotations or confirmations

Where you are required to submit a quotation or confirmation, ensure that you list all the service elements that you have extracted from the customer, together with the relevant benefits of your product or service.

Also consider where you put these in the actual quotation. Make sure that the benefits and service elements are the last thing that they read rather than the price which is a common failing. That is, show that the service and benefits justify the price.

Activity 21

Identifying buying and service motives

Prepare a plan to establish the services and buying motives for those customers who generate 80 per cent of your business.

- What do you want to establish?
- How can it be quantified?
- How will you record the information?
- How frequently will you review these with each customer?

Dealing with customer complaints

Even with the most structured and systemised service procedure and quality control, for many reasons something will go wrong and result in a customer complaint. If they do not complain, the problem can be far more serious and the result could be a move of allegiance to another supplier, without giving you the opportunity to rectify matters.

Before discussing how a customer complaint should be handled, it is worth while considering some of the most common reasons for customer complaints:

- Product or service fails to meet customer's expectations and needs.
- Delivery or completion date not as agreed or expected.
- Product or service did not measure up to verbal promise.
- Unreliable product or service.
- Hidden or unspecified costs.

Many, if not all, of these issues can be minimised, even avoided, by paying attention to detail and avoiding any misunderstanding of what customers want, ensuring that their expectations are compatible with what you are supplying.

Misrepresentation of your product or service is a serious offence and could have a costly or damaging impact on your company's credibility with far-reaching implications. However, even after all precautions have been taken, complaints will still occur.

The key point to remember is that customers' co-operation, attitude, flexibility and behaviour towards resolving the issue will not only be influenced by the final outcome, but also by the way that they are treated initially. This is the critical stage that can turn a complaint into a major crisis, generating anger, inflexibility and almost certainly a lost customer who may well seek to publicise the issue.

Stage 1

People's emotions are running high when something that they have purchased fails to function or does not meet their expectations. While resolving the problem is the ultimate aim, initially they require some-one to give them a sympathetic ear. Really listen to their problem. You are not required to concede every issue, just listen. In much the same way that a balloon shrinks when you let some of the contents blow out of it, so a complaint deflates when you let part of its pressure exhaust into words – when you let customers get off their minds what they have on them, without interruptions. Any interruption may be taken as a challenge to the individual and only serves to fan the flames of anger.

Even though they may make exaggerated statements, keep cool and show genuine interest with sympathetic body language. Eventually they will move into a more rational stage and may even start apolo-gising. Now you can start to deal with the complaint.

Stage 2

- Obtain all the facts.
- Establish what the customer is expecting.
- Do not agree to any action, unless you have the authority.
- Take notes and be seen to do so. This signals sincerity.
- Make a clear commitment to the customers of when you will report back to them. Good communications are crucial in resolving complaints.

Stage 3

Customer complaints will not go away, they will haunt you. Deal with them positively and you may well have a very loyal customer. The key is to keep the customer informed. Even if you do not have the final answer to resolving the complaint, report back on every agreed date, until the issue is resolved. Failure to keep the customer informed will only serve to aggravate the situation, harden attitudes and make the customer less likely to accept a potential compromise or apology. Once you have the answer, see or contact the customer at your earliest opportunity, and, where relevant, confirm your pro-posals in writing.

As acknowledged, problems do happen which result in dissatisfied customers. Having dealt with the complaint, the final stage is to analyse what caused the problem and what steps need to be taken to minimise the likelihood of this happening again.

Preventative action process:

- Identify all the causes.
- Involve all parties to discuss steps to be taken to minimise future occurrence. Do not waste time in apportioning blame. This will not solve anything.
- Agree joint strategy and action plan.

If relevant, you may even tell the customer what preventative actions have been put into place.

Remember, long after the complaint itself is forgotten, the customer will remember how you dealt with it.

Profiting from complaints

Research into complaints has highlighted some key facts:

- Customer complaints are a service opportunity.
- Most dissatisfied customers do not complain.
- A company needs to welcome complaints as a second chance to retain the customer.
- Every complaint made but not satisfactorily dealt with, makes the customer 20 per cent more likely to transfer the business. Just being able to complain helps.
- Credibility may not be restricted to the customer with the complaint. A customer who has had cause to complain will tell an average of nine or ten other people and many of those will also repeat the saga. The story will increasingly focus on how the customer was dealt with.
- When the person making the complaint has received a satisfactory response, he/she will tell only half the number of people and will talk about it positively.

Activity 22

Analysing service problems

Think of three instances where you have had cause to complain about a product or service.

- How did they handle your complaint?
- Have you subsequently returned and why?
- What are the key points from your experience?

Health and safety

The responsibility, knowledge and disciplines relating to all aspects of health and safety, have now been given a significant focus in all facets of the workplace. Your health, safety and welfare at work are protected by law. Your employer has a duty to protect you and to keep you informed about all aspects of health and safety. You have a responsibility to look after yourself and others and to comply with legislation and your company policy. Health and safety legislation is both wide-ranging and comprehensive, covering the following key areas:

- Factories Act 1961.
- Health and Safety at Work Act, etc. 1974.
- Health and Safety Display Screen Equipment Regulations 1992.
- Personal Protective Equipment at Work Regulations 1992.
- Manual Handling Operations Regulations 1992.
- Control of Substances Hazardous to Health 1994 – (COSHH).
- First Aid at Work 1981.
- Fire Regulations.
- Reporting of Injuries, Diseases and Dangerous Occurrences 1996 – (RIDDOR).

This is by no means a definitive list but an indication of the range of current legislation and more is likely to follow.

Your responsibility is to become aware of the knowledge that you need in relationship to your own company and its products and services including your liabilities.

One key point to remember: whenever you are on customer premises you are bound by their policy and procedures in all aspects of health and safety.

If you drive a vehicle in the course of your sales activity you need to be quite clear of your responsibilities as specified by your company and your obligations under the law.

All aspects covering health and safety at work are administered and controlled by a government body – the Health and Safety Executive.

There are area officers throughout the country who are only too pleased to offer advice and the Executive also publishes a range of informative books.

The Essentials of Health and Safety at Work ISBN 0 717 60716 X is an excellent starting point, covering the basic principles and how and where to go for further information.

The following self-test is by no means exhaustive, but is likely to be the minimum knowledge that you need to have to meet your health and safety obligations.

Activity 23

Health and safety questionnaire

Questions

1 If you have any suggestions on health and safety who do you address them to?

2 What does COSHH stand for?

3 What is meant by a control measure?

4 What does PPE stand for?

5 What does a black fire extinguisher contain?

6 What is a COSHH assessment used for?

7 What does a blue fire extinguisher contain?

8 What does a skull and cross bones on a chemical mean?

9 What two general rules should employed when lifting objects?

10 Who is responsible for health and safety at work?

11 What does a red fire extinguisher contain?

12 What does an 'X' mean on a hazardous product?

13 How would you lift a load that was awkward or extremely heavy?

14 Why should you not use a water fire extinguisher on an electrical fire?

15 Which accidents need to be put in the accident book?

16 When on customer's premises, whose health and safety policy applies?

17 Who are the Health and Safety Executive?

18 What is RIDDOR?

19 Who is your health and safety officer?

20 What is your company policy if involved in personal accident?

21 What is your company policy if involved in a motor vehicle accident?

22 What are your legal obligations if involved in a personal or motor vehicle accident?

See answers on p. 170

Activity 24

Health and safety when on customer's premises

Write a brief report on the requirements, precautions and safety discipline that you need to take in three different customer environments in which you are likely to be involved.

Answers to Activity 23

1 Line manager or member of health and safety committee.
2 Control of Substances Hazardous to Health.
3 How you handle the substance and storage.
4 Personal protective equipment.
5 CO_2 (used for liquid and electric fires).
6 Assessing potentially harmful products.
7 Dry powder (used for liquid and electrical fires).
8 The product is toxic or very toxic.
9 Straight back and bent knees.
10 Everybody.
11 Water (do not use on electrical fires).
12 The product is irritant or harmful.
13 Get help or use mechanical aids.
14 Risk of electric shock from the water allowing the electricity to track back.
15 All.
16 The customer's.
17 National body which monitors and administers all aspects of health and safety at work.
18 Reporting of Injuries, Diseases and Dangerous Occurences Regulations.
19 A nominated person within your company.
20 This should exist as a documented policy.
21 This should exist as a documented policy.
22 Refer to your company policy and the Highway Code.

National Vocational Qualification (NVQ) and Scottish Vocational Qualification (SVQ) in Sales Levels 2 and 3

NVQ and SVQ standards for Sales Levels 2 and 3

The NVQ and SVQ in Sales, developed and implemented by the Sales Qualification Board (the Lead Body for Sales and Sales Management), represent a landmark in recognising sales as a properly qualified profession.

The aim of this manual is to support the attainment of Levels 2 and 3 in Sales, both for the established salesperson and those who are beginning their careers in selling. It identifies the necessary attitudes, knowledge and skills that are the fundamental qualities of a successful professional salesperson.

Initially the terminology used in NVQs and SVQs may not appear to relate to all industries, for each industry by its nature is unique and has its own 'jargon'. However, regardless of what you are selling, these standards encapsulate the fundamental principles that all professional salespeople must meet if they are to achieve job satisfaction and their company's commercial expectations.

Every three years the standard is evaluated to ensure that it is in line with current practice and commercial trends.

Supporting notes in this manual will develop the attitude, knowledge and skills required and, together with the activities suitably endorsed by your line manager or assessor, will provide a practical way to build substantive evidence for your portfolio.

The NVQ and SVQ structure

All NVQs and SVQs are structured in a similar way. A series of units and elements become collectively a specific standard.

Units

Each NVQ and SVQ in Sales is a group of units which can be related to a specific level of sales responsibility and ability. Each unit is then subdivided into component parts called elements.

Elements

Each element is made up of three factors which need to be supported with evidence:

1 **Performance criteria**
   These are a specific number of standards of performance related to the element title.

2 **Range statement**
   A description of the different circumstances in which the competence has to be demonstrated.

3 **Underpinning knowledge**
   This outlines the supporting knowledge that is required for each element.

Each of the activities in this book can be used as evidence in meeting relevant performance criteria, range and underpinning knowledge.

Evidence

Substantiating evidence is required for every unit as previously outlined. This may be derived from many sources and providing it is factual it can be used as evidence.

Examples of types of evidence that can be used:

- Letters from customers.
- Letters from line managers.
- Letters from colleagues.
- Copy of correspondence to customers, managers, colleagues.
- Work plans.
- Call plans.
- Journey plans.
- Sales bulletins.
- Video/audio tapes.
- Actual or role-play simulations.
- Training reports.
- Appraisals.
- Copy proposals.
- Factual case study.
- Activity analysis.
- Customer records.
- Photographs.
- Observations.

NVQs and SVQs in Sales are competence based and therefore, wherever practicable, observed evidence in actual sales situations is preferable. Remember one piece of evidence often will support more than one element.

Quick reference guide

The following guide is intended as a quick reference for those using this book to support their NVQ or SVQ in Sales Levels 2 and 3. It indicates which notes and numbered activities primarily relate to specific units.

Unit 2   Forecast, Monitor and Evaluate Personal Sales Performance

Unit 3   Contribute to Effective Working

How to evaluate personal sales performance
Monitoring and forecasting
Health and safety principles and responsibilities

Activities: Preparing your own profile (1)
Analysing your own strengths and weaknesses (2)
Important principles of selling: self-analysis (3)
Identifying your key sales activities ratios and averages (14)
Health and safety questionnaire (23)
Health and safety when on customer's premises (24)

Unit 4   Contribute to and Maintain Systems, Procedures and Practices Which Support the Sales Function

Customer service
Dealing with customer complaints

Activities: Identifying buying and service motives (21)
Analysing service problems (22)

Unit 5   Maintain Effective Communication

Effective oral and written communication
Maintaining customer records

Unit 6   Identify and Generate Selling Opportunities

How to identify and create selling opportunities using the telephone to make appointments
Using the telephone to make appointments

Activities: Activity planning for prospective customers (18)
Introducing your company (19)

Unit 7 Conduct Sales

Call planning and preparation
Questioning techniques
Features and benefits
Dealing with and overcoming objections
Closing or gaining commitment
Visual sales aids

Activities: Establishing call objectives for existing and potential customers (4)
Planning questions to ask existing and potential customers (5)
Identifying the features and benefits of your company and its products (6)
Developing positive techniques for dealing with sales objections (7)
Analysing your closing techniques (8)
Developing your visual sales aids (11)

Unit 8 Plan and Organise Personal Work Schedule

Sales territory planning and management
Personal development action plan

Activity: Journey planning and customer analysis (20)

Unit 9 Make a Sales Presentation

Making effective group sales presentations

Activities: Using visual aids (12)
Presentation checklists (13)

Unit 10 Negotiate Sales

Principles and techniques of sales negotiation

Activities: Negotiation evaluation (9)
Negotiation planning (10)

Unit 11 Design and Implement a Sales Plan

Unit 22 Contribute to the Collection and Use of Marketing Information in Order to Meet Organisational Sales Objectives

How to prepare an area sales plan

Activities: SWOT analysis (15)
Hit list targeting (16)
Activity analysis (17)

Building your portfolio

The aim of the portfolio is to present in a logical sequence, evidence that demonstrates that you match each element of the standard. Suitable documentation to record your evidence will be supplied by the awarding body of your choice or you are fully entitled to use your own.

You are in fact in a sales situation, the objective is to construct and present a sales presentation on yourself:

- The needs have been identified – the standards.
- The benefits are – personal recognition.
- The close – you achieve an NVQ or SVQ.

> **Successful people do the things that unsuccessful people do not like doing.**

SALES NVQ AND SVQ LEVELS 2 AND 3 IMPLEMENTATION ACTION PLAN

Name ....

Section/Unit/Element ....

Date ....

Points for action in priority order	Activities required	Resources needed/ third party involvement	Completion by

Personal development action plan

Whether your aim is to achieve NVQ or SVQ Levels 2 or 3 or to develop your sales expertise, formulate and work to an implementation plan.

- Consider and decide:
  - in what sequence you aim to complete each section
  - what activities need to be implemented to complete each section and in what order
  - what resources you will require and why
  - who needs to be involved and why
  - when you aim to complete each section.
- Complete a detailed implementation plan for each section and for the whole manual.
- Remember plans are and must be working documents.
- Review on a planned basis and where necessary amend deadlines.
- Make the plan work for you.

Index

Note: Page numbers in **bold** refer to sample forms, checklists, diagrams etc.